THE LINGUISTIC RELATIVITY PRINCIPLE
AND HUMBOLDTIAN ETHNOLINGUISTICS

JANUA LINGUARUM

STUDIA MEMORIAE
NICOLAI VAN WIJK DEDICATA

edenda curat

C. H. VAN SCHOONEVELD

INDIANA UNIVERSITY

SERIES MINOR

NR. 67

1968

MOUTON

THE HAGUE · PARIS

THE LINGUISTIC RELATIVITY PRINCIPLE AND HUMBOLDTIAN ETHNOLINGUISTICS

A HISTORY AND APPRAISAL

by

ROBERT L. MILLER

McGILL UNIVERSITY

1968

MOUTON

THE HAGUE · PARIS

LIBRARY OF CONGRESS CATALOG CARD NUMBER: 68-13340

Printed in The Netherlands by Mouton & Co., Printers, The Hague

ACKNOWLEDGMENTS

The original version of this study served as a dissertation at the University of Michigan in 1963. The author is sincerely grateful to the members of his doctoral committee: Professors William P. Alston, William J. Gedney, Albert H. Marckwardt, and Herbert H. Paper, and especially to its chairman, Professor Herbert Penzl, for their suggestions and encouragement.

TABLE OF CONTENTS

INTRODUCTION

The relation of language to cognition has been one of man's most critical preoccupations. Indeed, some have taken the manner in which this relation is resolved to be a kind of cultural gauge for an epoch. In his book *Language and Reality* Wilbur Urban suggested that, if a history of European thought and culture were written from the standpoint of language, this history would be the story of two great opposing valuations – high and low evaluations of the WORD. A high evaluation of language, he wrote, recognizes the inseparability of the word and the thing; the knowable and language are in some degree identified. This attitude, he claims, is the mark of all positive cultural epochs. It is the underlying assumption of all periods of rationalism and is accompanied by some belief in the reality of universals, "since the very naming of anything immediately universalizes it in some sense and to some degree". A low evaluation of language, on the other hand, is indicated by a loosing of the word from the thing; the knowable is known independently of language. This attitude appears in all critical periods of culture. It underlies all periods of empiricism and is associated with a skepticism of the word, with a disbelief in universals. Urban characterized the critical periods as ones of skepticism, "since skepticism is always ultimately skepticism of the word", and cultural relativism. And of the five such critical turning points in Western European culture which he distinguished, Urban included the period in which we are now living.[1]

[1] Wilbur Marshall Urban, *Language and Reality* (New York, 1939), 22-32.

Although Urban pointed out that during the early part of the nineteenth century, the most recent 'high evaluation' period of language, a hypothesis was advanced which COMPLETELY identified reason with language, he failed to elaborate the significance of this hypothesis with respect to the question of universals. Whereas the empiricists had believed that the universalizing function of language actually veils or distorts sense data, which are the 'real' contents of cognition, and the rationalists had held that this function was at best a faithful witness to or an immediate product of reason, this later hypothesis maintained that the universals found in language constitute the very means by which we can know anything; knowledge is given exclusively through them.

Moreover, if our conception of things is somehow conditioned by the categories into which they are placed, and if the things placed in these categories vary from language to language, it follows that the 'same' phenomena, both sensory and nonsensory, will be conceived in different ways. This change in attitude toward the status of universals accounted in large measure for the new inference drawn as to the status of the individual languages: each language was said to contain a peculiar *Weltanschauung*, which causes its speakers to 'see' the world in a way different from the speakers of other languages. The earliest formulation of this conception of language, which has since come to be known as the 'linguistic relativity' hypothesis, is usually associated with the name of Wilhelm von Humboldt, but foreshadowings of it can be found in the writings of his immediate predecessors, Johann Georg Hamann and Johann Gottfried Herder.[2]

---

[2] It is interesting to note that the period in which the linguistic relativity hypothesis was being propounded coincides with that link in the great chain of being which Arthur O. Lovejoy has called "diversitarianism". Coming as a reaction to a longer period of "uniformitarianism", where the basic assumption was that "what is most important, most valuable, normal, in men consists in what is the same in all men", the assumption of diversitarianism, on the contrary, proclaimed that it is the diversity itself of "men and ages and peoples, in their ways of thinking and feeling and expressing themselves in arts and institutions" that is "'natural' and necessary, and also supremely desirable and right". A major consequence of this premise was that the *Eigentümlichkeit*, the characteristic feature,

Under the influence of Darwinian naturalism, however, the inseparability of *Geist* and *Sprache*, upon which Humboldt had insisted, was replaced by a tendency to regard language as but another episode in nature, as accompanying but not fundamentally altering our intuition of experience. It was not until the 1920's and 1930's in Germany that a small group of scholars, headed by Leo Weisgerber and Jost Trier, gradually revived Humboldt's hypothesis. At about the same time, and apparently independent of the German current, an American version of linguistic relativity was appearing. The hypothesis of linguistic relativity was probably introduced to America by Franz Boas,[3] became well known through its formulation by his student Edward Sapir,[4] and was vigorously defended in the writings of Benjamin Lee Whorf.[5]

It is especially Whorf's writings that have occasioned the recent controversy probing the validity of the hypothesis. The range of this controversy may be judged from the number of articles, conferences, projects, and experiments which linguists, philosophers, anthropologists, and psychologists have focused on the subject

---

that which sets one individual, nation, or race off from another, was sought and cultivated. Although this idea, Lovejoy writes, had a long prehistory it reached its climax in the 1790's among the original German Romanticists. Although Lovejoy does not mention language explicitly, for Herder, the chief spokesman of early German Romanticism, language was a nation's most characteristic possession, comprising its mentality and *Weltanschauung*. See Arthur O. Lovejoy, *The Great Chain of Being: A Study of the History of an Idea* (Cambridge, Mass., 1936), especially Lecture X. Cf. the same author's "The Meaning of Romanticism for the Historian of Ideas", *Journal of the History of Ideas*, II (June, 1941), 272-78.

[3] Claude Lévi-Strauss, Roman Jakobson, C. F. Voegelin, and Thomas A. Sebeok, *Results of the Conference of Anthropologists and Linguists* (*Indiana University Publications in Anthropology and Linguistics, Memoir* 8; Baltimore, 1953), 23.

[4] According to Hoijer, the Sapir-Whorf hypothesis probably had its initial formulation in two paragraphs of Sapir's article "The Status of Linguistics as a Science", first published in 1929. See *Language in Culture: Proceedings of a Conference on the Interrelations of Language and Other Aspects of Culture*, ed. Harry Hoijer (Chicago, 1954), 92.

[5] See *Language, Thought, and Reality, Selected Writings of Benjamin Lee Whorf*, ed. John B. Carroll (Cambridge, Mass., 1956).

within the past fifteen years.[6] The majority of these studies have been attempts to clarify or test the assumptions upon which the hypothesis rests.

The purpose of the present study will be to trace the course of the German version of the hypothesis, as it has appeared from Hamann to the present day. A major task of the study will be to illuminate the manner in which the German proponents of linguistic relativity have coped with their ultimate assumption: that reality is a 'flux of impressions'. The chief function of language, according to them, is to fix the contents of this flux for the consciousness and simultaneously to relate them to one another.

<hr />

[6] See especially: H. A. Bedau, Review of J. B. Carroll (ed.), *Language, Thought, and Reality*, in *Philosophy of Science*, XXIV (1957), 289-93; Ludwig von Bertalanffy, "An Essay on the Relativity of Categories", *Philosophy of Science*, XXII (October, 1955), 243-63; Max Black, "Linguistic Relativity: The Views of Benjamin Lee Whorf", *The Philosophical Review*, XLVIII (April, 1959), 228-37; Roger Brown, "Linguistic Determinism and the Part of Speech", *Journal of Abnormal and Social Psychology*, LV (1957), 1-5; Roger Brown and Eric H. Lenneberg, "A Study in Language and Cognition", *Journal of Abnormal and Social Psychology*, XLIX (1954), 454-62; John B. Carroll, "Linguistic Relativity, Contrastive Linguistics, and Language Learning", *International Review of Applied Linguistics in Language Teaching*, I (1963), 1-20; John B. Carroll and Joseph B. Casagrande, "The Function of Language Classifications in Behavior", in *Readings in Social Psychology*, eds. Eleanor Maccoby, Theodore M. Newcomb, and Eugene L. Hartley (3rd ed.; New York, 1958), 18-31; Joseph B. Casagrande, "The Southwest Project in Comparative Psycholinguistics: A Preliminary Report", in *Men and Cultures*, ed. Anthony F. C. Wallace (Philadelphia, 1960), 777-82; Lewis S. Feuer, "Sociological Aspects of the Relation Between Language and Philosophy", *Philosophy of Science*, XX (April, 1953), 85-100; Joshua A. Fishman, "A Systematization of the Whorfian Hypothesis", *Behavioral Science*, V (October, 1960), 323-39; J. H. Flavell, "A Test of the Whorfian Hypothesis", *Psychological Reports*, IV (1958), 455-62; Raymond D. Gastil, "Relative Linguistic Determinism", *Anthropological Linguistics*, I (December, 1959), 24-38; Paul Henle, "Language, Thought, and Culture", in *Language, Thought, and Culture*, ed. Paul Henle (Ann Arbor, 1958), 1-24; Hoijer (1954); Eric H. Lenneberg, "Cognition in Ethnolinguistics", *Language*, XXIX (July-September, 1953), 463-71; Eric H. Lenneberg and J. M. Roberts, *The Language of Experience* (*Indiana University Publications in Anthropology and Linguistics, Memoir* 13; Baltimore, 1956); Lévi-Strauss *et al.* (1953); G. A. Radnitzky, "Some Remarks on the Whorfian Hypothesis", *Behavioral Science*, VI (1961), 153-57.

Humboldt, under Kant's influence, explicitly called attention to this dual role of language when he said that the inflected languages, in 'purely' distinguishing between the conceptual and relational components of language and thought, expressed most clearly "the purpose of language, which perpetually divides and connects, and of the nature of thought itself".[7] Humboldt's present-day followers have, like Humboldt, based their claim that each language influences its speakers to see and think in a characteristic way on the premise that the 'conceptual partition of the world' and the manner in which this 'partition' is organized is different in each language.

---

[7] Wilhelm von Humboldt, *Gesammelte Schriften*, ed. Albert Leitzmann (Berlin, 1903-1918), VII, 263. Unless otherwise indicated all translations throughout this study are my own.

1. HAMANN, HERDER, HUMBOLDT

Rudolf Unger has shown that Johann Georg Hamann was the first writer in Germany to deal with the question of the influence of language on thought.[1] In accordance with the basic assumption of rationalism language was generally regarded at the time as a mere appendage of reason, as the tool of an autonomous and uniform consciousness. The assumption of a *gemeinen Menschenverstand*, the faculty of perception said to be possessed by all normal persons, and which is completely independent of language, accounts for the interest shown at the time in "universal" grammars and languages. Since language was the product of reason, the conviction arose that, beneath the diverse forms which the historic languages display, there could be discovered a 'universal' language, one which would ideally represent the concepts of the mind.

But Hamann, as the result of a religious conversion in 1758, became convinced that language, far from being a mere tool or conscious product of reason, entered into the very structure of cognition, was a constitutive factor in its development. Although Hamann's belief in the priority of language over reason is usually found expressed in its GENERAL form, there are nevertheless passages in his writings which deal explicitly with the question of linguistic relativity. However, due to both Hamann's well-known

[1] *Hamanns Sprachtheorie im Zusammenhange seines Denkens* (Munich, 1905), 214. For a recent re-evaluation of Hamann's theory of the relation of language to cognition, see James C. O'Flaherty, *Unity and Language: A Study in the Philosophy of Johann Georg Hamann* (*University of North Carolina Studies in the Germanic Languages and Literatures*, No. 6; Chapel Hill, N.C., 1952).

aversion to system and his adoption of an aphoristic style of writing, a clear interpretation of this problem in Hamann can best be obtained by examining the general principles of his philosophy.

Perhaps most of what Hamann has to say about the relationship of language to thought can be derived from his belief in the divine origin of language.[2] Just as in the beginning when God called the world into being through the divine Logos, so man too, having been taught this miracle by God, re-creates his own spiritual reality by means of human language:

Every phenomenon of nature was a word, – the sign, symbol, and pledge of a new, secret, inexpressible, but all the more intimate union, communication, and community of divine energy and ideas. Everything that man heard in the beginning, saw with his eyes, contemplated, and touched with his hands, was a living word; for God was the Word. With this word in his mouth and in his heart, the origin of language was as natural, as near, and as easy as child's play.[3]

What is important in understanding Hamann in this connection is that language is regarded by him as spontaneous and necessary expression.[4] Language and reason occur simultaneously, and where a logical distinction is made between them language always comes first. Language is an *Urfaktum*, a primitive, representing an indissoluble unity, and historically inexplicable.[5] Four years before his death, in a letter to Herder, he writes:

[2] Cf. Urban, 71-72: "From the beginning reflection upon languages has been preoccupied with origins ... the questions of the nature, function, and limits of language are still answered in terms of their supposed origin."

[3] Johann Georg Hamann, *Sämtliche Werke*, ed. Josef Nadler (Vienna, 1949-53), III, 32. References to Nadler's edition will hereinafter be inserted parenthetically into the text and will be indicated by N. A Roman numeral is used to designate the volume number, an Arabic numeral to designate the page number.

[4] See Ernst Cassirer, *The Philosophy of Symbolic Forms*, trans. Ralph Manheim (New Haven, 1953), I, 150-51; Fritz Heinemann, *Wilhelm v. Humboldts Philosophische Anthropologie und Theorie der Menschenkenntnis* (Halle/Saale, 1929), xviii.

[5] See Erwin Metzke, *J. G. Hamanns Stellung in der Philosophie des 18. Jahrhunderts* (Halle/Saale, 1934), 127; Fritz Blanke, "Gottessprache und Menschensprache bei J. G. Hamann", *Theologische Blätter*, IX, No. 8 (August, 1930), col. 206.

Even if I were as eloquent as Demosthenes, I would have to do nothing more than repeat a single maxim three times: reason is language, λόγος. On this marrow I gnaw and will gnaw myself to death on it. For me a darkness still hovers over these depths; I am still waiting for an apocalyptic angel with a key to this abyss.[6]

With his emphasis on immediate impression as the source of all true knowledge, we can readily understand Hamann's conviction that the language of parable and of everyday experience, and not the abstract language of philosophers, is the real bearer of meaning:

The Scriptures cannot speak with us as human beings otherwise than in parables, because all our knowledge is sensory, figurative, and because understanding and reason make the images of external things everywhere into allegories and signs of more abstract, more intellectual concepts. [N, I, 157-58; cf. N, I, 18; N, I, 112; N, II, 197.]

Hamann's conviction that "all our knowledge is sensory, figurative" brought him into direct conflict with Kant. The crowning point of this conflict was Hamann's answer to Kant's *Critique of Pure Reason*, the "Metacritique Concerning the Purification of Reason" (1784). In this essay, Hamann takes up the problem raised by Kant as to whether knowledge of external objects is possible without or before sensuous impressions. In claiming the autonomy of reason over "experience and its everyday induction" (N, II, 284), Kant ran counter to the very grain of the Hamannian philosophy. For Hamann, the most direct and immediate form of experience was not reason, as he believed Kant to be saying, but language:

If it therefore still remains a principal question as to how the capacity to think is possible – the capacity to think, to the right of and to the left of, before and without, with and beyond experience, no deduction is necessary to establish the genealogical priority of language and its heraldry over the seven sacred functions of logical propositions and conclusions. Not only does the entire capacity to think rest on language, ... but language is also the center of the misunderstanding of reason with itself. ... [N, II, 286.]

[6] Johann Georg Hamann, *Schriften*, eds. Friedrich Roth and Gustaf A. Wiener (Berlin, 1921-43), VII, 151-52.

Hamann would thus reverse Kant's assumption of the "receptivity of language and spontaneity of concepts" (N, III, 284).

The manner in which words combine their sensuous and logical properties is described by Hamann as a "hypostatic union", whereby the meaning and designation of words

arise ... from the combination of a word-sign, which is *a priori* arbitrary and indifferent, but *a posteriori* necessary and indispensable, with the perception of the object itself. And through this repeated bond the concept is communicated to, engrained upon, and embodied into the understanding by means of the word-sign rather than by means of the perception itself. [N, III, 288.]

It is obvious from the foregoing that Hamann's conception of reason calls for a definition different from that found in Kant. The latter defines reason (*Vernunft*) as "the capacity which gives the principles of knowledge *a priori*" (*Critique of Pure Reason*, 2, 53). For Hamann, reason does not function as an independent faculty of cognition, as he believed it did for Kant, "but rather is fertilized by the Logos and is solely the capacity for deriving concepts from sensory impressions, and for forming judgments and conclusions" (N, VI, 394, item "Vernunft").

But since, according to Hamann, sensory impressions are given to us only through language, reason itself is not merely an abstraction, but must be relative to the particular language one speaks. In a letter to Jacobi, he writes: "Our conceptions of things are modified in a new language, in another system of signs, which bring new relationships to mind, or rather restore the ancient, original, true ones." [7] Gründer has summarized Hamann's position in this matter thus:

Language as such ... is never simply general, but rather is always the specific language. ... Each language, ... represents its own world, is bound up, ... with all thinking and realizes, as its base and support, the presence of reason in historic existence. No more than there is

[7] Johann Georg Hamann, *Briefwechsel mit Friedrich Heinrich Jacobi*, ed. C. H. Gildemeister (Gotha, 1868), V, 494. Cf. also: "In another philosophy, in another religion, another language is unavoidable; other conceptions, other names for the same objects which everyone designates from the viewpoint of his necessity or spontaneity." *Ibid.*, 516.

thought free of language, is there a suprahistorical and ahistorical reason.[8]

But if reason is determined by language, or at least if it does not 'cause' language, Hamann elsewhere recognizes an element which CAN influence language, and which at the same time modifies his claim that language is an *Urfaktum*. In his early "Essay Concerning an Academic Question" (1760), Hamann had claimed that

natural mentality (*natürliche Denkungsart*) has an influence on language. Both universal history as well as the history of individual peoples, societies, sects, and persons, a comparison of several languages with that of a single one in the various relationships of time, place, and content all serve to furnish an ocean of observations which a learned philosopher could organize into simple principles and general classes. If our conceptions (*Vorstellungen*) dispose themselves according to the mind's viewpoint, and if, as many believe, the latter is determined by the state of the body, then the same thing can be applied to the body of a whole people. The lineaments of their language will thus correspond to the direction of their mentality; and every people reveals its mentality through the nature, form, laws, and customs of its speech as well as through its outward culture and through a pageant of visible behavior. [N, II, 122.]

The 'natural mentality' of a speech community gives rise to what Hamann calls the "genius of a language".[9] His definition of 'genius', however, tells us little:

This natural disposition (*Naturell*) of a language must be mistaken neither for grammar nor rhetoric; just as little as the likeness of a painting is due exclusively either to the symmetry of the design or to the mixing of the colors, or of light and shadow, but rather is independent of both. [N, II, 123.]

[8]   Karlfried Gründer, *Figur und Geschichte: Johann Georg Hamanns "Biblische Betrachtungen" als Ansatz einer Geschichtsphilosophie* (Freiburg, 1958), 189.

[9]   According to Cassirer, the first explicit formulation of a 'spirit of language' is to be found in Book 3, Chapter 5 of Harris' *Hermes* (1751): "we shall be led to observe how Nations, like single Men, have their *peculiar* Ideas; how these *peculiar* Ideas become THE GENIUS OF THEIR LANGUAGE ..." Cassirer, 144-45.

But language, on the other hand, can also influence 'mentality'. The example adduced by Hamann, however, is again inconsequential: the freedom of an author writing in his native language is contrasted with the bondage of one writing in a foreign language (N, II, 126).

Hamann's explicit statements regarding linguistic relativity are admittedly sparse, the most important argument in Hamann in support of the idea that each language creates its own conceptual world being the implicit one derived from the general principles of his philosophy. He seemed too preoccupied, in his struggle to reverse the basic assumptions of Kant and the Enlightenment, to develop his own theory in detail. Even when he is engaged in discussing concrete questions about grammar or orthography, one senses his real concern – to help clarify the mystery of the 'original datum', Language.[10] In this respect Hamann reveals himself as a child of the Enlightenment. Leo Weisgerber, in describing the change from Hamann to Herder, writes:

If the thoughts of the Enlightenment revolved more around the question: what is language?, there was now imperceptibly shoved into its place the more concrete question: what is a language? This step can even be observed in the relationship of Hamann to Herder. It is really the projection of language into historical reality.[11]

Cassirer has shown how the influence of two such widely different minds as Hamann and Leibnitz contributed to Herder's theory of the origin of language.[12] But it can also be shown how Herder wove elements from both thinker's philosophies into the whole fabric of his philosophy of language.

Being a former student of Hamann's and thus standing in close contact with his ideas, Herder deepened and enlarged his teacher's attacks against the Enlightenment's conception of language as a tool or product of reason. Herder's most concentrated blow to this

[10] See Metzke, *loc. cit.*: Hamann speaks of the "variable scheme of all language" (N, II, 172) and the "metamorphosis of language" (N, II, 248).
[11] *Von den Kräften der deutschen Sprache*, IV: *Die geschichtliche Kraft der deutschen Sprache* (2d ed. rev.; Düsseldorf, 1959), 210.
[12] Cassirer, 152-53.

conception was occasioned by a controversy into which both he and Hamann entered. In 1759 the Berlin Academy of Sciences interrupted its traditional inquiry into metaphysical problems, and offered a prize instead to the best answer to a question dealing with language: *Quelle est l'influence réciproque des opinions du peuple sur le langage et du langage sur les opinions?* The prize was awarded in May of the same year [13] to the famed Orientalist Johann David Michaelis for his essay, "Über den Einfluss der Meinungen auf die Sprache und der Sprache auf die Meinungen". Weisgerber has indicated how clearly the commentary to the competitive question reflected the attitude of the Enlightenment toward language.[14] It was hoped that by examining the 'strange' (*bizarre*) turns of expression found in a language, and showing how they favor or obstruct the search for the 'true ideas' a means might be found to improve the 'inadequacies' of languages. Although Michaelis' prize essay itself was of little further moment for linguistics, it did provoke the opposition of Hamann [15] and Herder.

Herder's response is to be found in the first book of his completely revised "Fragments Concerning Modern German Literature" (1768).[16] In this work Herder begins by accepting Hamann's thesis that language and reason are identical, fully conscious of the deterministic implications of such a doctrine:

If words are not merely signs, but also, as it were, the moulds in which we see our thoughts, then I would regard a whole language as a great range of thoughts having become manifest [S, II, 12]. . . . If it is true that we cannot think without thoughts, and that we learn to

[13] Weisgerber has noted how opportune the question must have been, since it did not, as was often the case, require years for a satisfactory answer to be submitted. See Weisgerber, *Von den Kräften der deutschen Sprache*, III: *Die Muttersprache im Aufbau unserer Kultur* (2d ed. rev.; Düsseldorf, 1957), 7.

[14] *Ibid.*, 8.

[15] See Hamann's "Essay Concerning an Academic Question" (1760).

[16] Johann Gottfried Herder, *Herders Sämtliche Werke*, ed. Bernhard Suphan (Berlin, 1877-1913), II, 1-108. References to Suphan's edition will hereinafter be inserted parenthetically into the text, and will be indicated by S.

think through words, then language gives to the whole of human knowledge its limits and contours [S, II, 17]. ... We think in language ... and in ordinary life it is indeed apparent that thinking is almost nothing more than speaking [S, II, 18]. ... Thus I would regard language as the tool, the content, and the form of human thoughts [S, II, 24].[17]

In regarding language as the "tool, the content, and the form of human thoughts", Herder concluded that language is man's most characteristic work, and that an examination of the different languages of the earth is the best contribution toward a "philosophy of the human understanding" (S, XV, 183):

Every nation speaks ... according to the way it thinks, and thinks according to the way it speaks: As varied as the viewpoint was from which a nation looked at a thing, it designated it the same way. [S, II, 18; cf. also S, II, 25; S, I, 6.]

Every language, then, being the reflection of a 'national mentality', corresponds to the structure and content of this mentality. Herder thus applies to language the same principle which he does to every other form of human culture – the Leibnitzian principle of individuation.

In his *Monadology*, Leibnitz had declared:

This bond or adaptation of all created things to each, and of each to all, causes every simple substance to have relations which express all the others, and consequently each created monad is a perpetual living mirror of the universe. As one and the same city looked at from different sides appears different and presents innumerable aspects, so likewise it comes about that there are as many different universes as there are simple substances the multitude of which is infinite. All these different universes are, however, only perspectives of one universe from the different view-points of each monad.[18]

Just as each monad represents the universe as seen from its own perspective, so each language, being the supreme expression of a

---

[17] Compare also: "There is no condition of the human mind which is not capable of linguistic expression or not really determined by words of the mind." (S, V, 100.)
[18] Gottfried Wilhelm Leibnitz, *The Monadology*, trans. R. Latta and G. M. Duncan (London, 1930), 98-99.

'national mentality', in fact, identical with it, reflects the universe in its own characteristic way. Language is, for a nation, a "mirror of its history, deeds, joys, and sorrows" (S, XVII, 337).

Indices of a 'national mentality' are revealed according to Herder, through the 'idiotisms' (*Idiotismen*), a term he borrowed from Hamann. They are the distinctive features of a language, its 'patronymic charms'. Thus, the 'heaps' of consonants in German are said to give the language the "distinct, firm step, which never tumbles over, but rather strides with grace, like a German" (S, II, 31). He sees a similar analogy in German syntax: "And in the concatenation and inner sequence of our periods we can observe the gait of a German, ... to whom a uniform, steady, and manly gait is peculiar" (S, II, 44).

In his essay "Concerning the Origin of Language" (1772), Herder attributes the diversity of languages and their corresponding differences in mentalities to the variables of climate, time, and place;[19] and where totally diverse languages are found side by side, Herder believes a "mutual family and national enmity" to be in operation.[20]

Thus Herder, influenced by Leibnitz[21] and the emerging science of biology, interlaces the concepts of growth and development into his philosophy of language. Language is the "development of reason", the "formation of human mental powers" (S, II, 68), and Langen has pointed out how many metaphors taken from botany make up Herder's dynamic-organic view of the world.[22] Just as the various forms of plant life are explained

---

[19]   In attempting to correlate linguistic structure with geophysical and geographical features, Herder espouses a theory held by others before him: The "Universal History" of Ibn Khaldun (1332-1406); Huarte de San Juan, *Examen de ingenios para las ciencias* (1575); Francis Bacon, *De dignitate et augmentis scientiarum* (1623); Montesquieu, *L'esprit des lois* (1748); Johann Popowitsch, *Untersuchung vom Meere* (1750).

[20]   In his later treatise, "On the Cognition and Feeling of the Human Soul" (1778), Herder derives differences in manners of thinking from differences in manners of feeling (S, VIII, 210), which in turn depend on differences in 'character' (S, VIII, 226).

[21]   See Rudolf Haym, *Herder nach seinem Leben und seinen Werken* (Berlin, 1877), I, 185.

[22]   E.g., 'tree', 'flower', 'bud', 'seed', 'to grow'. See August Langen,

partly by adaptation to environment, so the diverse languages reflect the varied historic, geophysical, and psychological conditions under which they are spoken.

Thus Herder, in contrast to Hamann, finds the origin and development of language determined exclusively by psychological and natural forces, feeling that the concept of the divine origin of language presupposes the existence of an ideal language beside which all other languages are anomalies (S, II, 67).

In his essay on the origin of language, Herder gives his version of how language must have been 'invented'. This was achieved, so Herder's argument runs, by virtue of the specific human faculty of 'reflection' (*Besonnenheit*):

Man demonstrates reflection when the force of his soul works so freely that in the ocean of sensations that flows into it from all the senses, he can, in a manner of speaking, isolate and stop One wave, and direct his attention toward this wave, conscious that he is so doing. He demonstrates reflection when, emerging from the nebulous dream of images flitting past his senses, he can concentrate upon a point of wakefulness, dwell voluntarily on One image, observe it calmly and lucidly, and distinguish characteristics proving that this and no other is the object. He demonstrates reflection when he not only knows all attributes vividly and clearly, but can *recognize* one or more distinguishing attributes: the first act of this recognition yields a clear concept; it is the soul's First judgment – and what made this recognition possible? A characteristic which he had to isolate and which came to him clearly as a characteristic of reflection. Forward! Let us cry εὕρηκα! The first characteristic of reflection was the word of the soul. With it human speech was invented! [23] [S, V, 34-35.]

As an example of the exercise of reflection, Herder recalls how the lamb must have appeared to primitive man for the first time. The lamb stands before man, white, soft, and woolly, "just as it is presented to the senses". Man's mind, free from the distractions of animal instinct, looks for a characteristic feature (*Merkmal*). The sheep bleats! The mind

---

"Deutsche Sprachgeschichte vom Barock bis zur Gegenwart", *Deutsche Philologie im Aufriss*, ed. Wolfgang Stammler, I (Berlin, 1952), col. 1255.
[23] Quoted by Cassirer, 152-53.

has found a characteristic. The inner sense is at work. This bleating, that makes a strong impression on the mind, that tore itself away from all the visual properties, leaped forth, broke in deeply on the consciousness, and adheres in the mind. The sheep returns. White, soft, woolly – the mind sees, gropes, reflects, searches for a characteristic – the sheep bleats and now the mind recognizes it again! "Ah! you are the bleating one!" it feels. The sheep has been recognized by the mind in a manner characteristically human. This is because the mind recognizes and names the sheep distinctly, that is, with a *Merkmal*. . . . And what was that, if not an inner cue? The sound of bleating, perceived by a human mind as the distinguishing attribute of the sheep, became, by virtue of the faculty of reflection, the *name* of the sheep. And this, even if his tongue had never tried to stutter it. He recognized the sheep by the bleating, it was a sign (*Zeichen*) he understood and which caused the mind to reflect clearly on an idea – what is that, if not a word? And what is all of human language, if not a collection of such words? [S, V, 35-36.]

Although Herder did not in this essay indicate how differences in the choice of *Merkmale* show up in the various languages, he elsewhere suggests how instructive it is to compare the manner in which the various languages form substantives, for "not only does such a comparison point out the varied character of their inventors, but also the varied sides of things, which could be perceived, and the *motives of the designation* itself" (Herder's italics; S, XXI, 102-3).

Herder outlines the areas where 'differences' and its degrees among languages show up:

The act of giving names . . . varies everywhere on earth, even in designating audible things, indeed in the direct expressions of emotion – the interjections. In manners of perception or cold observation this diversity grows still more, and in metaphorical expressions, the figures of speech, and finally in the structure of language, in the relation, order, and concord of the parts to one another it is almost infinite. [S, XIII, 363-64.]

He suggests that a "people's genius reveals itself nowhere better than in the physiognomy of its speech":

Whether, for example, a people's language has many names or expresses much action? how it expresses person and tense? which order of concepts it favors? all this is often extremely characteristic. Many nations have a separate language for the two sexes. In others class distinctions even show up in the simple word *I*. Active peoples have an abundance of verbal moods; cultivated nations a number of expressions for the qualities of things which raised them to abstractions. [S, XIII, 364.]

In calling for a "general physiognomy of peoples as revealed in their languages", Herder was anticipating the work of the most prolific exponent of this thesis during the nineteenth century, Wilhelm von Humboldt. But Humboldt began with an assumption totally different from that of Herder. Whereas Herder, following Hamann, had rejected Kant's *Critique of Pure Reason* partly because he thought Kant failed to deal adequately with the problem of language, Humboldt, on the other hand, accepted Kant's theory of knowledge, but sought to add to its validity by applying the principles of Kant's concept of objectivity to the problem of language.[24] Cassirer describes in general terms at what point in Kant's philosophy this application took place:

What characterizes this [Kant's] concept of objectivity above all is the realization that an object of cognition can only be spoken of in connection with a *function* of cognition, and as being correlative to it. The object, as an object of knowledge, as an object of appearance, is not determined "in itself," but rather its determination grows progressively with the productivity of the mind. The direction of this productivity – the categories, which in this endeavor of the mind are determinative and operative – this gives rise to the new transcendental concept of objectivity. And there is ultimately, according to Kant, one single primary function within which this total endeavor can be encompassed. Forming the basis for all comprehension, for all determination of a concrete object as such, is the synthesis of judgment. The unity and the necessary connection of multiplicity which we have in mind when we speak about an "object of conceptions," goes back to the logical "unity of action," which is carried out by the function of judgment. Only by virtue of the judgments of quantity, of quality, of relation, does conceptualization acquire true universality and necessity, and is thereby transferred to the sphere of "being," to the realm

---

[24]   See Rudolf Haym, *Wilhelm von Humboldt: Lebensbild und Charakteristik* (Berlin, 1856), 447; cf. Ernst Cassirer, "Structuralism in Modern Linguistics", *Word*, I (August, 1945), 116.

of objectivity. It was at this point of critical epistemology that Humboldt's new theory of the philosophy of language took hold. What is here described by Kant as a feat of judgment, is shown by Humboldt to be possible in the concrete life of the mind only through the mediacy of speech. The objectification of thought must pass through the objectification of the speech sound.[25]

Language is for Humboldt what the synthesis of judgment is for Kant: a creative act of the mind. Just as synthesis for Kant is not the mere uniting of previous 'givens', but rather determines the nature of the constituents themselves, so language for Humboldt is not the mere appending of words on ideas detached from these words, but rather enters into the cognitive process itself. Humboldt repeatedly emphasizes this heuristic power of speech. "Language, in the individual word and in connected speech, is an act, a truly creative action of the mind." [26] And in this act of synthesis language itself becomes an object to the consciousness, and produces an effect upon it:

Concept and sound, connected in a manner in accordance with their own true essence, and knowable only in the fact itself, are expressed as word and speech, and in this way something different from both is created between the outer world and the mind [L, VII, 211]. . . . The mind creates, sets, however, the created by the same act opposite itself, and causes it, as an object, to react upon itself [L, VII, 213].

Language comes into being when thought, formless at first and struggling for clarity, becomes embodied in sound:

Language is the formative organ of thought. Intellectual activity – thoroughly psychic, internal, and, so to speak, flitting by without a trace – becomes, through the sounds of speech, externalized and perceptible to the senses. It and language are therefore one, and inseparable from one another. It is, however, by its very nature forced to enter into union with the speech sound; thinking cannot otherwise attain to clarity, nor can conception (*Vorstellung*) become concept (*Begriff*). [L, VII, 53.]

[25]   Ernst Cassirer, "Die Kantischen Elemente in Wilhelm von Humboldts Sprachphilosophie", *Festschrift für Paul Hensel* (Greiz i.V., 1923), 117-18.
[26]   Wilhelm von Humboldt, *Gesammelte Schriften*, ed. Albert Leitzmann (Berlin, 1903-1918), VII, 211. References to Leitzmann's edition will hereinafter be inserted parenthetically into the text, and will be indicated by L.

And from the physical property alone of speech sounds, an immeasurable advantage is gained for the mind. Through their mediacy the continuous flux of experience becomes ordered:

The cutting edge of the speech sound is indispensable for the mind in grasping objects. Both the things in external nature as well as the activity generated from within crowd in upon man with an array of features. He, however, strives for comparison, separation, and connection, and, in his loftier aims, for the formation of a more and more comprehensive unity. Thus he desires to grasp objects in a certain unity, and summons the unity of the sound to take its place. [L, VII, 54.]

In this manner words are formed:

From the mass of indeterminate and, as it were, formless thought a word pulls out a certain number of features, connects them, gives them form and color through the choice of sounds, through a connection with other related words, and through the addition of accidental secondary modifications. In this way the features are individualized by the word. [L, IV, 248.]

The word itself is the minimal unit capable of expressing the content of language:

In segmenting the content of language we can only go as far back as the word. ... The word possesses unity and definite shape, inwardly through the concept which it expresses, outwardly through its sound and accent. The word stands, by affinity and descent, in relationship with other words and can propagate its species beyond itself. [L, IV, 20.]

But, for Humboldt, language is not just a "collection of words," as Herder had claimed.[27] In his essay "Concerning the Comparative Study of Languages in Relation to the Various Ages of Language Development" (1820), Humboldt dwells at length on the notion that the most general and pervasive characteristics of language are articulation and structure (*Gliederung*). "The dominant principle in all language is articulation, and the most im-

---

[27] However, see Jost Trier, "Das sprachliche Feld. Eine Auseinandersetzung", *Neue Jahrbücher für Wissenschaft und Jugendbildung*, X (1934), 429: "It is interesting to see how Herder (II, 12ff.) wavers indecisively between the structural image and the simple stockroom image, arrested by the old stockroom conception, but tending towards the spatialized ideas of structure, which alone makes comprehensible what he wishes to say."

portant excellence of every language is fixed and flexible structure"
(L, IV, 17).

Humboldt employed the term 'articulation' to describe the
process by which the formless thought-mass and the equally
formless sound-mass, in their mutual striving for clarity, meet
and become ordered into the components of language:

> Man possesses the power to divide these territories, mentally by reflec-
> tion, physically by articulation, and to rejoin their parts, mentally by
> the synthesis of the understanding, physically by the accent, which
> unites the syllables to the word, and the words to speech [L, IV, 4.]

Though he does so only figuratively, Humboldt applies to language the Romantic concept of the organism. Language is not
a mere piling up of discrete elements, but rather takes place all
at once:

> Language cannot help but arise all at once, or, to be more exact, it
> must have in its possession at every moment of its existence that
> which makes it into a whole. As the immediate exhalation of an
> organic entity in its sensory and psychic capacities, language partakes
> of the nature of everything organic, so that every element in language
> exists only by virtue of the others, and everything only through the
> power penetrating the whole. [L, IV, 3.]

To a degree, then, with every utterance he makes, a speaker's
whole language is present to him:

> Language can be compared to a gigantic web, in which there is a
> more or less clearly recognizable connection between each part and
> the other, and between all parts and the whole. In speaking, man, no
> matter where he begins, always touches but a part of this web. He
> does this, however, instinctively, as though all parts, with which
> every single part must necessarily stand in agreement, were present to
> him all at once [L, VII, 70; cf. L, IV, 14-15]. . . . Since the union of
> the simplest concepts sets in motion the whole web of the categories
> of thought: since the positive presupposes and gives rise to the nega-
> tive; the part, the whole; unity, multiplicity; the effect, the cause;
> reality, possibility and necessity; the conditional, the unconditional;
> one dimension of time and space, the other; every degree of feeling,
> the one closest to it; so it is that, as soon as the expression of the
> simplest union of ideas has been established with clarity and precision,
> a totality exists in the language, according to the richness of the

vocabulary. Everything expressed elicits the unexpressed, or paves the way for it. [L, IV, 3-4.]

Any examination, therefore, into the structure of language must begin not with the word, but rather with the language as a whole:

It is impossible to think of language as originating with the designation of objects by words and then proceeding to their organization. In reality, speech is not put together out of words which preceded it, but on the contrary, words issue forth from the whole of speech. [L, VII, 72.]

According to Humboldt, the act of creative synthesis that takes place in thought and speech reveals its unity not in the word, but in the sentence. "Even in the sentence it [the essence of language] lies, as far as grammatical form goes, in perfect unity" (L, IV, 3). Although the synthetic process is found unified in the sentence, it actually informs the whole of language, merely showing up most clearly in the sentence:

It [synthesis] is most clearly recognized in sentence formation, then in words formed by inflection and affixes, finally in every nexus of concept and sound. [L, VII, 213.]

Furthermore, the synthetic act differs from language to language. "In every language this act is an individual one, behaving in every respect in a definite manner" (L, VII, 211). Humboldt believed that the inflected languages above all parallel most closely the 'natural' cognitive processes. Inflection "awakens ... by its inherent regard for the forms of thought, in so far as these relate to language, a more accurate and lucid insight into their nexus" (L, VII, 119).

But it is in words in their capacity for designating concepts that the most noticeable differences show up among the various languages. This led Humboldt to his well-known pronouncement:

The interdependence of word and idea shows us clearly that languages are not actually means of representing a truth already known, but rather of discovering the previously unknown. Their diversity is not one of sounds and signs, but a diversity of world perspectives (*Weltansichten*) [L, IV, 27]. ... As the individual sound does between the object and man, so the whole language intervenes between him and a nature reacting internally and externally upon him. ... Man lives with objects chiefly, indeed, since his feeling and conduct depend on his conceptions (*Vorstellungen*), solely as his language presents them to him. [L, VII, 60.]

This does not mean that there is not a denominator, however insignificant, common to all languages:

The attempt has indeed been made to substitute the words of the various languages by signs which are generally valid, like those which mathematics possesses in its lines, numbers, and algebra. But only a small part of that which is capable of being thought can thereby be exhausted, for these signs, by their very nature, correspond only to such concepts which can be generated by mere construction, or which are otherwise formed purely by the understanding. Where, however, the matter of inner perception and feeling is to be stamped as concepts, then it depends on man's individual capacity for conceptualization, from which his language is inseparable. All attempts to place visual or audible signs which would be generally valid at the center of the various languages are but abridged methods of translation, and it would be a foolish fancy to imagine that one could thereby step, I do not say out of all language, but at least out of the definite and limited circle of one's own. To be sure, a midpoint, around which all languages revolve, can be sought and really found, and this midpoint should always be kept in mind in the comparative study of languages, both in the grammar and lexicon. For in both there is a number of things which can be determined completely *a priori*, and which can be separated from the conditions of a particular language. On the other hand, there is a far greater number of concepts, and also grammatical peculiarities, which are so inextricably woven into the individuality of their language that they can neither be kept suspended between all languages on the mere thread of inner perception, nor can they be carried over into another language without alteration. A very significant part of the content of every language is therefore so unquestionably dependent on that language, that the language's expression for this content can no longer be a matter of indifference. [L, IV, 21-23.]

According to Humboldt, then, it is very seldom that a word in one language has its exact equivalent in that of another. This happens rarely in the designation of physical objects; it is even more rare in designating intellectual concepts:

If, in the various languages, we compare the expressions for non-physical objects, we will find only those synonymous which, because they are pure fabrications, cannot contain anything more or different than what has been placed in them. All other expressions cut up the territory lying in their midst, if we may so name the object designated by them, in different ways, and contain fewer, more, or different determinations. The expressions for material objects are probably synonymous in so far as the same object is thought of when they are used, but because they express a definite manner of conceiving (*vorstellen*) the object, their meaning (*Bedeutung*) likewise varies. [L, IV, 28-29.]

Humboldt offers an example of what he means, by comparing different designations for the same object within the same language:

When, for example, in Sanskrit the elephant is sometimes called the twice-drinker, othertimes the double-toothed-one, othertimes still the one-provided-with-a-hand, many different concepts (*Begriffe*) are designated, even though the same object is meant. For language does not represent objects, but rather the concepts which, in the process of speech, have been formed by the mind independent of those objects. [L, VII, 89-90.]

It is perhaps instructive to contrast Humboldt's position on this point with that of John Locke. Locke too, in his *Essay Concerning the Human Understanding* (1690), had held that there was almost never a complete correspondence in every range of meaning between the words of one language and those of another. But, for Locke, words are a mere means of expressing concepts already known independently of language; with Humboldt words aid in the discovery of concepts not yet known.

It should, however, be recognized that by the term 'diversity of world perspectives' Humboldt is espousing a linguistic, and not a philosophical relativism.[28] Language is "the human being approaching the objective idea" (L, V, 9):

The sum of the knowable lies, as the field to be tilled by the human mind, in the middle of, between, and independent of all languages. Man cannot approach this purely objective realm other than through his cognitive and sensory powers, that is, in a subjective manner. [L, IV, 27.]

[28]   See Leo Weisgerber, "Relativismus in Humboldts Sprachbetrachtung?", *Das Gespräch: Blätter der Freunde des Pädagogischen Verlags Schwann Düsseldorf*, Ausgabe A, Folge 2 (Frühjahr, 1953), 3-4.

And man's cognitive and sensory powers depend ultimately on the language he speaks.

Humboldt, like Herder, believed that the different linguistic structures were but reflections of the varied mental characteristics of their speakers. "A people's mental characteristics and language structure are so closely fused that, if the one were given, the other could be wholly derived from it" (L, VII, 42). There is another factor, however, which is the cause of both:

Without, however, wishing to decide on the priority of the one over the other, we must regard as the real explanation and the true reason for linguistic diversity the intellectualized energy (*geistige Kraft*) of nations. It alone stands vividly independent before us; language, on the other hand, is only attached to it. [L, VII, 42.]

And since, according to Humboldt, differences in the world perspectives of languages are measured in terms of a language's capacity for intuiting the 'objective realm', this capacity will "depend in general on the energy of intellectualized activity, and especially on the latter's characteristic inclination to form thought by means of sound" (L, VII, 254-55).

Because language is not merely "the impress of a people's ideas", but rather "their total intellectualized energy, transformed as if by magic into particular sounds" (L, VII, 602), any definition of language must take into account its intrinsically dynamic character. Humboldt's famous definition of language occurs in his last and best-known essay, "Concerning the Diversity of Man's Linguistic Structure and Its Influence on the Spiritual Development of the Human Race" (1830-1835):

Language must be regarded not so much as a dead product, but far more as a producing. One must disregard more those factors which cause language to be thought of as the designation of objects and as the vehicle of the understanding [L, VII, 44]. . . . Language viewed in its true essence is something perpetually, and in every moment, transitory. Even its preservation in writing is but an imperfect mummified storing away, which still requires one to sensualize the living speech. Language itself is not a work (*ergon*), but rather an activity (*energeia*). Its true definition can, therefore, only be a genetic one. Language is properly the ever repeated effort of the spirit to form the articulated sound into an expression of thought. Strictly speaking, this is the definition of each actual speech-occurrence, but in a true and fundamental sense only the totality of speech, so to speak, can be regarded as language. [L, VII, 45-46.] [29]

The formative principle which organizes this energy into a systematic whole is what Humboldt calls the 'inner form' of a language:

What constitutes form in language is that enduring and uniform element, conceived as perfectly as possible in its inner coherence, and systematically depicted, which is present in this effort of the mind to elevate the articulated sound to an expression of thought. [L, VII, 47.]

Humboldt believes that all those features, from the phonology, to the grammar, to the individual peculiarities of designation contained in the lexicon, that distinguish one language from another can be referred back to the operation of that language's inner form. Thus, it is the dynamics of a language's inner form that determines its peculiar world perspective.

We may say in summary that, although Humboldt, in contrast to Hamann and Herder, accepted the Kantian theory of epistemology, he was led into agreement with Humann and Herder on a major point: that the more immediate forms of experience are 'given' to man through language, and, furthermore, that each language presents these forms in a different way. Though only alluded to or present by deduction in Hamann, this hypothesis becomes consciously formulated in Humboldt's dictum "that words and syntax form and determine concepts, and that, observed in their connection and their influence on cognition and

[29] Cf. Cassirer's comment on Humboldt's *ergon/energeia* dichotomy: "Language is neither a mechanism nor an organism, neither a dead nor a living thing. It is no thing at all, if by this term we understand a physical object. It is – language, a very specific human activity, not describable in terms of physics, chemistry, or biology. The best and most laconic expression of this fact was given by W. v. Humboldt, when he declared that language is not an *ergon* but an *energeia*." Cassirer (1945), 110. For the evolution of Humboldt's energeia concept, see Leonhard Jost, *Sprache als Werk und wirkende Kraft: Ein Beitrag zur Geschichte und Kritik der energetischen Sprachauffassung seit Wilhelm von Humboldt (Sprache und Dichtung*, 6) (Bern, 1960).

feeling, the several languages represent in fact several world perspectives" (L, IV, 420). The two factors that give the hypothesis its meaning at this stage, and which serve as starting points for later investigations are Herder's *aperçu* that 'recognition' is only possible through the word-sign in its function of meaning, and Humboldt's claim that language is a system of such signs.

2. SAUSSURE, CASSIRER

During the remaining part of the nineteenth century we encounter but sporadic traces of Humboldt's ideas regarding linguistic relativity,[1] and these add little or nothing to Humboldt's original theory. The discovery of Sanskrit and the influence of Darwin encouraged an almost exclusive interest in historical phonetics and morphology, studies more suited to a comparative and evolutionary approach than are the studies dealing with the relationship between language and cognition. Influenced by Darwin, the majority of linguists regarded language as part of nature, as a tool to aid man in adapting himself to his environment but not as fundamentally altering his conception of that environment. Under this view language itself came to be explained in the same terms as nature, namely, as following certain physical or physiological 'laws'. Later, an increasing interest in semantics, coupled with the gradual rise of modern psychology, caused this conception of language to be displaced by a psychological one. But according to this strictly psychological interpretation, language was still regarded as part of nature, for the processes of the mind were conceived in purely mechanical terms.[2] This conception of language is especially evident in Wilhelm Wundt's *Völkerpsychologie*. For although Wundt included in this work a comprehensive theory of language, it is obvious that he merely uses

---

[1] See, for example: Wilhelm Scherer, *Zur Geschichte der deutschen Sprache* (Berlin, 1868); Franz Nikolaus Finck, *Der deutsche Sprachbau als Ausdruck deutscher Weltanschauung* (Marburg, 1899).
[2] Cf. Urban, 30-31 and 59-61.

language to confirm the concepts of sensation, perception, idea, intuition, and so on, which had already been defined in his work on physiological psychology; language is still thought of primarily as a secondary reflection of these concepts.

In both the physical or physiological and the psychological approaches toward language, then, the epistemological identity between language and thought which Humboldt had emphasized was in general lost sight of. Whereas Humboldt had maintained that the world of 'things' is constructed and acquires meaning only through language, the assumption of these later approaches was that the world of 'things' is already constructed without the aid of language; the problem was to find out how it acquires meaning and is known. This assumption is present even in Whitney, who otherwise recognizes Humboldt's concept of inner form:

> Every single language has thus its own peculiar framework of established distinctions, its shapes and forms of thought, into which, for the human being who learns that language as his "mother tongue," is cast the content and product of his mind, his store of impressions, however acquired, his experience and knowledge of the world. This is what is sometimes called the "inner form" of language – the shape and cast of thought as fitted to a certain body of expression.[3]

Furthermore, the idea that the material substance of language is merely an addendum to its conceptual content, a content which is ORIGINALLY the same for the speakers of all languages, explains the general neglect of Humboldt's notion of the organological structure of language; for Humboldt had stressed the interdependency of all elements within a language ON THE PREMISE THAT THE CONCEPTUAL CONTENT OF EACH ELEMENT DETERMINES THE CONTENT OF ALL OTHERS.

There was, however, a growing awareness that there are certain systems of meanings within a language which belong together, and that the full meaning of an element depends on the position it occupies within the system to which it belongs, the most important contributions of this kind were Hermann Osthoff's book on

[3] William D. Whitney, *The Life and Growth of Language* (New York, 1880), 21-22.

suppletion [4] and R. M. Meyer's article on military titles.[5] Meyer claimed, for instance, that the meaning of 'major' could only be derived from knowing that it came between 'captain' and 'lieutenant-colonel', and so forth.[6]

It was not until the advent of what Gunther Ipsen has called the "new speech notion" [7] that an atmosphere congenial to the acceptance of Humboldt's ideas once again appeared. What is significant about this 'speech notion' for the present study is its phenomenological postulate that the ultimate key to language is found in meaning, and not in 'things' or in psychic mechanisms; language and meaning are both conceived as descriptive ultimates, not explainable in terms of physics, physiology, or even psychology. According to Ipsen the new speech notion has been most closely associated with the names of Edmund Husserl and Ferdinand de Saussure.

Husserl, in attempting to construct a 'pure logic', had insisted that, however imperfect, a close nexus exists between natural language and the realm of 'ideal unities', that the objects which fall under the investigation of 'pure logic' are given chiefly in 'grammatical garb'.[8] In his analysis of the linguistic expression (*Ausdruck*) contained in the *Logischen Untersuchungen*, he declared that "the essence of the expression lies exclusively in meaning (*Bedeutung*)",[9] and that the meaning of an expression remains "the same no matter who expressed it as an assertion,

---

[4] Hermann Osthoff, *Vom Suppletivwesen der indogermanischen Sprachen* (Heidelberg, 1899).
[5] Richard M. Meyer, "Die militärischen Titel", *Zeitschrift für Deutsche Wortforschung*, XII (1910), 145-56.
[6] Cf. Stephen Ullmann, *The Principles of Semantics* (2d ed. rev.; Oxford, 1957), 154-55.
[7] See Gunther Ipsen, *Sprachphilosophie der Gegenwart* (Berlin, 1930), 11-21; the same author, "Der neue Sprachbegriff", *Zeitschrift für Deutschkunde*, XLVI, No. 1 (1932), 1-18; cf. Fritz Stroh, "Allgemeine Sprachwissenschaft und Sprachphilosophie", in *Germanische Philologie: Ergebnisse und Aufgaben. Festschrift für O. Behaghel* (Heidelberg, 1934), 229-42; Urban, 62ff.
[8] Edmund Husserl, *Logische Untersuchungen* (2d ed. rev.; Halle, 1921), II, 1, 29.
[9] *Ibid.*, 49.

and under whatever circumstances and time he does it".[10] "Never," he insists further, "does the object coincide with its meaning"; [11] the "linguistic expression designates (*bezeichnet, nennt*) the object *through* its meaning".[12] Meaning in Husserl's system, then, is independent of what the private psychological state of the individual is. Although 'intended' (*intendiert*) through psychic acts, meaning is by no means exhausted in them; meaning rather has an objective and unalterable validity of its own.

But although meaning in Husserl's system is freed from a psychologistic bias, by attributing an independent status to meaning Husserl was at the same time denying that the formal and conceptual differences in linguistic expression among languages reflect differences in cognition:

The meaning which belongs to the word-sound, and the act of cognition in which the meaning is at the moment united with that which is meant, is maintained everywhere unaltered, so that the differences must obviously pass as insignificant.[13]

Thus, although the Humboldtians accepted Husserl's thesis that the essence of linguistic expression is meaning and that this meaning is the same for everyone, they repudiated his claim that differences in expression among the individual languages do not signify differences in cognition.[14]

In Saussure the Humboldtians found a spirit very much akin to their own. The Geneva linguist in fact expressly reaffirmed some of Humboldt's most fundamental conceptions of language. One of these was the concept of ARTICULATION:

Psychologically our thought – apart from its expression in words – is only a shapeless and indistinct mass. Philosophers and linguists have

---

[10] *Ibid.*, 43.
[11] *Ibid.*, 46.
[12] *Ibid.*, 49.
[13] *Ibid.*, 2, 29.
[14] See especially: Walter Porzig, "Der Begriff der inneren Sprachform", *Indogermanische Forschungen*, XLI, No. 2 (1923), 162-63; Leo Weisgerber, "Sprachwissenschaft und Philosophie zum Bedeutungsproblem", *Blätter für deutsche Philosophie*, IV (1930), 33-39; Fritz Stroh, *Der volkhafte Sprachbegriff* (Halle, 1933), *passim*.

always agreed in recognizing that without the help of signs we would be unable to make a clear-cut, consistent distinction between two ideas. Without language, thought is a vague, uncharted nebula. There are no pre-existing ideas, and nothing is distinct before the appearance of language. ... The characteristic role of language with respect to thought is not to create a material phonic means for expressing ideas but to serve as a link between thought and sound, under conditions that of necessity bring about the reciprocal delimitation of units. Thought, chaotic by nature, has to become ordered in the process of its decomposition. Neither are thoughts given material form nor are sounds transformed into mental entities; the somewhat mysterious fact is rather that "thought-sound" implies division, and that language works out its units while taking shape between two shapeless masses. ... Language might be called the domain of articulations. ... Each linguistic term is a member, an *articulus* in which an idea is fixed in a sound and a sound becomes the sign of an idea.[15]

For Saussure, then, as for Humboldt, thought and language are inseparable:

Language can ... be compared with a sheet of paper; thought is the front and sound the back; one cannot cut the front without cutting the back at the same time.[16]

Saussure made a sharp distinction between the grammatical and phonological structure of a specific language (*la langue*), and the temporal process of speech transmission (*la parole*) in which the language is actualized by its speakers. He pointed out that although each individual has his own way of speaking he must stay within certain fixed boundaries set by the grammatical and phonological structure of his language if he is to be understood by other members of his speech community. Saussure thus emphasized the sociological reality of language, its supraindividual status. Language is a code, so to speak, which is collectively operative in the brain of every member of a speech community.

The linguistic sign (*signe*) itself consists of two components: the signified (*signifié*), that is, the concept, and the signifier (*signifiant*), that is, the sound-image. *Signification* is the psycho-

[15] Ferdinand de Saussure, *Course in General Linguistics*, trans. Wade Baskin (New York, 1959), 111-13.
[16] *Ibid.*

logical process whereby the concept and the sound-image are brought into relation with one another. As Humboldt before him had done, Saussure too stresses the systematic character of linguistic signs; in doing so he introduces his concept of value (*valeur*):

> Language is a system of interdependent terms in which the value of each term results solely from the simultaneous presence of the others.[17]

Letting what is said of a word be equally valid for any and every entity in a synchronous system, Saussure makes a sharp distinction between the value and the signification of a word. Signification is a word's property of standing for a concept, and in this sense the word may be said to possess value, that is, it may be exchanged for a given concept. But, in addition, a word must be compared with the similar significations, the values in the narrow sense, of other words standing in opposition to it; it is this comparison with words of similar value that gives a word its own value:

> Its [a word's] content is really fixed only by the concurrence of everything that exists outside it. Being part of a system, it is endowed not only with a signification but also and especially with a value, and this is something quite different.[18]

A reciprocal delimination, then, determines the value of words expressing related ideas. This can be illustrated by comparing words within the same language or among different languages. As an example of the latter:

> Modern French *mouton* can have the same signification as English *sheep* but not the same value, and this for several reasons, particularly because in speaking of a piece of meat ready to be served on the table, English uses *mutton* and not *sheep*. The difference in value between *sheep* and *mutton* is due to the fact that *sheep* has beside it a second term while the French word does not.[19]

For Saussure, then, meaning (*le sens*) is determined by both the signification and the value of linguistic units, and he concluded

---

[17]   *Ibid.*, 114.
[18]   *Ibid.*, 115.
[19]   *Ibid.*, 115-16.

that "if words stood for pre-existing concepts, they would all have exact equivalents in meaning from one language to the next".[20] That this is not true is shown not only by the lack of complete correspondence of values among the words of different languages, but among their grammatical entities as well. For example, the value of a French plural does not coincide with that of a Sanskrit plural even though their signification is usually identical; this is because Sanskrit has three numbers instead of two. Saussure points to distinctions of time, as in Hebrew, and aspect, as in the Slavic languages, which are not formally indicated in other languages. Calling attention to the lack of a special form for the future in Proto-Germanic, he observes: "To say that the future is expressed by the present is wrong, for the value of the present is not the same in Germanic as in languages that have a future along with the present." [21]

It is clear from the foregoing that a new definition must be found for the concepts that arise from the mutual interaction of thought and sound:

Instead of pre-existing ideas then, we find in all the foregoing examples *values* emanating from the system. When they are said to correspond to concepts, it is understood that the concepts are purely differential and defined not by their positive content but negatively by their relations with the other terms of the system. Their most precise characteristic is in being what the others are not.[22]

According to Saussure there are two basically different ways of viewing language. These may be symbolized by two intersecting co-ordinates: a horizontal 'axis of simultaneities' and a vertical 'axis of successions'. The former describes the SYNCHRONISTIC appproach, which views language as a system of coexisting relations; the latter represents the DIACHRONISTIC approach, which deals with linguistic phenomena as they develop in time. Saussure insists that the two approaches must be kept strictly apart, and that values are relevant only with synchronous systems.

It would be difficult to overestimate Saussure's influence on

[20] *Ibid.*, 116.
[21] *Ibid.*, 117.
[22] *Ibid.*

the later Humboldtians. Leo Weisgerber and Jost Trier, the fore-most representatives of this group, have everywhere acknowl-edged the Geneva linguist's contribution to their own theories [23] and it is evident in most of their most fundamental conceptions. Saussure's pervasive influence is explained partly by the precision with which he defined many of the notions which had been sug-gested merely in metaphor or aphorism by Humboldt.[24] Although the incompatibility which Saussure had claimed exists between the synchronistic and diachronistic approaches was later chal-lenged by the Humboldtians, his distinction between the signifi-cation and value of linguistic units provided the Humboldtians with a workable theory for defining more precisely their basic premise: that each language influences its speakers to "see" dif-ferently than the speakers of other languages. For, according to the Humboldtians, values are determinative in the cognitive process itself. And since the values of linguistic units rarely cor-respond in every respect from one language to the next, it follows that the 'same' phenomena will not be experienced in the same way by the speakers of two different languages. A fuller discus-sion of this proposition will be taken up later.

In the year 1923 two publications appeared which might be regarded as heralding the beginning of the Neo-Humboldtian revival: the first volume, dealing with the relation of language to cognition, of Ernst Cassirer's *Philosophy of Symbolic Forms*; and an article on Humboldt's concept of inner speech form, written by the Indo-European scholar Walter Porzig.[25]

---

[23]   In a private conversation with Peter Hartmann, Weisgerber asserts that the two men that have most decisively shaped his thought have been Saussure and Cassirer. See Peter Hartmann, *Wesen und Wirkung der Sprache im Spiegel der Theorie Leo Weisgerbers* (Heidelberg, 1958), 20. For Trier's acknowledgment of Saussure's influence on the former's con-ception of the linguistic 'field', see especially Jost Trier, *Der Deutsche Wortschatz im Sinnbezirk des Verstandes: Die Geschichte eines sprach-lichen Feldes* (Heidelberg, 1931), 11.
[24]   Cf. Jost Trier, "Über die Erforschung des menschenkundlichen Wort-schatzes", in *Actes du Quatrième Congrès International des Linguistes* (Copenhagen, 1938), 93-94.
[25]   Porzig (1923).

Porzig, though adding little to the substance of Humboldt's original concept, at least reinstated it within the framework of an idealistic philosophy of language. Porzig agrees in particular with Humboldt's claim that the morphological and syntactical forms of a given language influence its speakers. These forms (called by Porzig 'meaning-forms' [*Bedeutungsformen*], collectively the 'outer form' of a language) condition an individual speaking that language to "a priori forms of apperception" [26] which differ from those experienced by speakers of other languages. These forms represent a unity because they are the immediate products of a single, immanent form-giving principle. The proof that there is a single unifying principle and that this principle is present in every speaker of a given language is shown, according to Porzig, by a language's ability to generate new forms; these forms, although not spoken or heard before, are immediately understood by members of the community speaking that language. Porzig defines inner speech form, then, as "the peculiar apperception-forms of a speech community which stand in reciprocal relation with its outer speech form".[27]

Porzig claims that the world picture of a language can only be rendered intelligible if its meaning-forms are "adequately grasped in their essence and peculiarity",[28] and if the observer's findings are not prejudiced by the mode of intuition of his own language. Although no analysis of this kind has yet been carried completely through for any language, Porzig points to some differences in meaning-forms which might serve as starting points for such an investigation:

We can for example say that the speakers of the ancient Indo-European languages perceived (*apperzipierten*) action only according to the forms of "progress" and "completion"; that in Classical Latin every event is perceived (*wahrgenommen*) chiefly according to the form of its *temporal* relation within the total content of consciousness; that what we call the "subject of action" appears in the modern Indic

[26] *Ibid.*, 165.
[27] *Ibid.*, 167.
[28] *Ibid.*, 166.

vernaculars (and under their influence also in Classical Sanskrit) rather as the cause of an event, etc.[29]

Even within the same speech community meaning-forms (and with them their apperception-forms) change in the course of time. The transition for example from a 'synthetic' to an 'analytic' stage is indicative of a change in cognition.

In his contribution to the volume commemorating Wilhelm Streitberg a year later,[30] Porzig defined linguistic meaning (*Bedeutung*) as "nothing more than the property of the sign (*Zeichen*) to intend (*meinen*) the real".[31] He thus proposed a definition of meaning which, like Husserl's, makes meaning independent of private psychic states but which, UNlike Husserl's, makes meaning dependent on the linguistic sign for its validity. Whereas for Husserl linguistic expressions designate objects THROUGH a realm of meanings 'existing' independently of these expressions, for Porzig meaning is 'given' and 'exists' only through linguistic expression. Porzig distinguished between the meaning-contents (*Bedeutungsinhalten*) and the meaning-modes (*Bedeutungsweisen* − called *Bedeutungsformen* in his previous article) of language:

When we talk about meaning we usually have only meaning-*content* in mind. Nevertheless, at least as important for linguistics is the form of meanings, the manner and mode in which an expression intends (*meint*) a content. One and the same meaning-content, for example *Caesar*, can be given in different forms. In the sentences *Brutus murdered Caesar* and *Caesar was murdered by Brutus, Caesar* intends each time, in the strictest sense of the word, the same content. Nevertheless, there is a difference for linguistics, and, indeed, a difference which pertains essentially to the sphere of meaning; the content *Caesar* is intended in two very different ways, namely, first as object, then as subject. These different manners and modes, in which an expression can intend the same fragment of reality, I call *meaning-modes*. *Meaning-modes*, then, are for example subject and predicate, object and attribute, as well as substantive and adjective, concrete and abstract, perfect and imperfect, etc. To employ a metaphor: while the

[29] *Ibid.*
[30] "Aufgaben der indogermanischen Syntax", in *Stand und Aufgaben der Sprachwissenschaft: Festschrift für W. Streitberg* (Heidelberg, 1924), 126-51.
[31] *Ibid.*, 137.

meaning-*content* fixes the direction, so to speak, in which a telescope is focused, the meaning-*modes* correspond to the differently ground and tinted lenses which I can insert in this telescope.[32]

The meaning-modes, the combinations into which the meaning-contents can enter, are for Porzig "the fundamental forms of our world picture".

But it was Cassirer's imposing interpretation of the symbolic function of language contained in the first volume of his *Philosophy of Symbolic Forms* that lent tremendous support to the hypothesis of linguistic relativity.[33] Influenced by Humboldt himself, Cassirer's tome was studded with references to Humboldt's writings. But especially significant was Cassirer's attempt to show that language, far from being a mere secondary or derivative construct, is in fact present from the very beginning, is determinative in the perceptual process itself. To show what role language plays in perception, Cassirer pointed to the growing realization on the part of logicians, especially Sigwart and Lotze, that the generic concepts arrived at in formal logic depend ultimately on a universalizing process present already in language: [34]

In the usual logical view, the concept is born only when the significa-tion of the word is sharply delineated and unambiguously fixed through certain intellectual operations, particularly through "defini-tion" according to *genus proximum* and *differentia specifia*. But to penetrate to the ultimate source of the concept, our thinking must go back to a deeper stratum, must seek those factors of synthesis and analysis, which are at work in the process of word formation itself, and which are decisive for the ordering of all our representations according to specific linguistic classifications.[35]

[32]   *Ibid.*, 132-33.
[33]   Although not reckoned among the Neo-Humboldtians, Cassirer, at least in his *Philosophy of Symbolic Forms*, seems to have espoused the linguistic relativity notion. He later, however, seems to have abandoned the idea. See Eric H. Lenneberg, "A Note on Cassirer's Philosophy of Language", *Philosophy and Phenomenological Research*, XV (June, 1955), 512-22. Cassirer was conspicuously silent about the activities of the Neo-Humboldtians.
[34]   See Cassirer (1953), chap. iv; cf. also Urban, 141ff.; Urban, "Cassirer's Philosophy of Language", in *The Philosophy of Ernst Cassirer* (New York, 1949), 414-16.
[35]   Cassirer (1953), 280.

Lotze had pointed out how, after we have performed a series of logical operations to determine the content of a general concept, for example *blue* or *color*, we have still not explained where the generic *blue* 'exists', under which we subsumed light blue or dark blue, or the generic *color*, under which we subsumed red and yellow:

The common factor in red and yellow, by virtue of which they are both colors, cannot be detached from what makes red red and yellow yellow; that is to say, this common factor cannot be detached and made into the content of a third representation of the same kind and order as the other two. Our sensation communicates only a particular color shade, a particular pitch, volume and quality of tone. . . . Anyone who wishes to apprehend the universal in color or tone will inevitably come up against the fact that what he has in mind is the intuition of a specific color or sound accompanied by the reflection that every other tone or color has an equal right to serve as an intuitive example of the universal which is itself not subject to intuition; or else, his memory must present many colors and tones successively, while again he reflects that what he is seeking is not these particulars but that which is common to them and which cannot be intuited in itself.[36]

To describe this primary formation found in language, Lotze coined the term 'first universal' to distinguish it from the 'second universal' of traditional logic. But as Cassirer pointed out, these two universals have little more than the name in common; they, in fact, represent two distinct KINDS of structure:

The relation of subsumption, which traditional logic regards as the constitutive relation through which the universal is connected with the particular, the genus with the species and individuals, is not applicable to the concepts which Lotze designates as the "first universal." Blue and yellow are not particulars subordinated to the genus "color in general"; on the contrary, color "as such" is contained nowhere else but in them and in the totality of other possible color gradations, and is thinkable only as this aggregate in its graduated order. Thus universal logic points to a distinction which also runs through the whole formation of linguistic concepts. Before language can proceed to the generalizing and subsuming form of the concept, it requires another, purely *qualifying* type of concept formation. Here a thing is not

[36]   *Ibid.*, 282.

named from the standpoint of the genus to which it belongs, but on the basis of some particular *property* which is apprehended in a total intuitive content. . . .[37] The beginning of thought and speech is not this: we do not simply seize on and name certain distinctions that are somewhere present in feeling or intuition; on the contrary, on our own initiative we draw certain dividing lines, effect certain separations and connections, by virtue of which distinct individual configurations emerge from the uniform flux of consciousness.[38]

To fix the impressions in the ever-moving stream of consciousness, then, the mind, in the act of concentrating on this stream, abstracts, that is 'names', properties which are common to several individual phenomena. But these properties are not only characterized by a 'whatness' which enables us to recognize again as the 'same' the total intuitive content to which it belongs, as in the case of Herder's lamb, they are also ORDERED into groups and series which themselves are properties of more comprehensive totalities: not only can the various shades, tones, and other properties of color phenomena function as instances of blue, yellow, and other colors, but 'blue' and 'yellow' themselves are special instances of 'color as such', and so on.

According to Cassirer, then, the different conceptual categories into which the same sensory phenomena are placed by different languages reflect differences in perception. "If the moon in Greek is called the 'measurer' (μήν), in Latin the 'glittering' (*luna, lucna*), we have here one and the same sensory intuition assigned to very different notions of meaning and made determinate by them."[39] To denote the specific law whereby each language, as set off from others, effects its concept formation Cassirer invokes Humboldt's term 'inner form'. Although, according to Cassirer, Humboldt used the term ambiguously, applying it sometimes to the laws of grammatical combination, other times to the origin of 'word-root' significations, Cassirer claims that it is primarily in the latter sense that Humboldt intended it to be taken.

Three years after Cassirer's volume on language appeared,

---

[37] *Ibid.*, 283.
[38] *Ibid.*, 280.
[39] *Ibid.*, 284-85.

Leo Weisgerber again took up the question of inner speech form.[40] As though to corroborate the paramount position Cassirer ascribed to language in the construction of the perceptual world, Weisgerber referred to the recent investigations performed by Gelb and Goldstein in the field of psychopathology.[41] These investigations dealt with patients having speech disturbances due to brain damage, particularly those suffering from amnesic aphasia. Especially affected among such patients was their ability to group or name colors. Although it was proved that the patient's optical faculty was unimpaired (he was, in fact, capable of making the finest color distinction), he could not react normally to common color names. If for example he was asked to pick out from a pile of skeins of different colors all the red or blue skeins, including the various shades of these colors, or if he was shown a skein of, say, a dark red, and then asked to match it with skeins of the same or similar color, he seemed not to understand or else began sorting the skeins into what at first seemed like a meaningless group. It became evident, however, that the patient, not understanding the generic names 'red' or 'blue', had arbitrarily settled upon a sensuous property of the model skein, say, its intensity, brightness, tonality, or the like, and had tried to sort the other skeins according to this property. But even here the patient was not always consistent, often slipping from one form of classification into another, from say, intensity into brightness. If asked to name the color of a particular skein, the patient used such terms as strawberry-red, sky-blue, grass-green, white as snow, and the like; the color was always used in connection with a named object.

The patient's behavior thus differs characteristically from that

[40] Leo Weisgerber, "Das Problem der inneren Sprachform", *Germanisch-Romanische Monatsschrift*, XIV (1926), 241-56.

[41] A. Gelb and K. Goldstein, "Über Farbennamenamnesie", *Psychologische Forschung*, VI (1925), 127-86. For a more recent statement of their findings see Kurt Goldstein, "On Naming and Pseudonaming, from Experiences in Psychopathology", *Word*, II, 1 (1946), 1-7; consult also the same author's *Language and Language Disturbances* (New York, 1948). Cassirer also utilized Gelb and Goldstein's researches in the third volume of his *Philosophy of Symbolic Forms* (1929).

of a normal person. The normal person, if required to choose all skeins that are red, groups together skeins showing varying nuances of brightness, tonality, and the like; in other words, the nuances are not taken as things in themselves, but as instances of the color category redness. Thus, the normal person is guided by a definite active ordering principle which is lacking in the patient.

But Gelb and Goldstein point out that another approach is open to the normal person. If, for example, the normal person starts with one particular skein and passes it over the heap, passively surrendering himself to the emerging impressions, one of two things will take place:

The colors that are identical with the model will immediately cohere in a unitary sensory experience, even the colors that exhibit a close similarity to the most striking attribute of the model. If, however, there are in the heap no colors which, like the identical ones, cohere with the model in all respects, but only in some, then the result is an *alternation in the intuitive union of colors.* But even at the time when we are considering as passively and cursorily as possible the heap of skeins, we are experiencing something similar; the heap appears restless, agitated, and we notice a continual alternation, a kind of rivalry among groupings according to the different attributes.[42]

The patient, then, is continually in the condition in which the normal person is only when the latter regards the heap passively. Gelb and Goldstein called this the concrete attitude. The 'conceptual' or 'categorical' attitude, whereby the normal person regards the concrete color as a representative of a certain color category, is called the abstract attitude.

Cassirer's theory that the categorical function of language is actually bound up with the perceptual process itself seemed to be empirically confirmed for Weisgerber by Gelb and Goldstein's researches into aphasia. That sensory phenomena are experienced according to the category to which they are assigned, forms the very bedrock of Weisgerber's hypothesis:

If man, in the face of the infinite multiplicity of phenomena, is to attain to an "objective" attitude, then he must create for himself rally-

42   Gelb and Goldstein, 151.

points to which he can, by the process of conceptual assimilation, refer the newly appearing impressions and events. *What serve as points of crystallization for concept formation are, above all, linguistic symbols*; the latter are, then, to emphasize explicitly once again, *not external appendages* which are attached purely associatively to concepts acquired in some other way, but rather they are *constitutive elements* which are just as important in fixing an individual event as in assimilating the event into the totality of previous experiences. On concepts thus acquired depends man's categorical behavior, that is, his looking at things not as individual phenomena, but as representatives of conceptually coherent complexes.[43]

According to Weisgerber, then, language, by forcing us to assign impressions and events to its ready-made categories, does our thinking FOR US so to speak. In stressing the supraindividual character of language Weisgerber sounded a theme which was to run through all of his later writings:

If we put ourselves completely in the position of the experiencing and concept-forming person, the concept "red" is acquired not so much through the person's recognizing something common in the differently shaded color experiences as it is through the fact that the common linguistic symbol, under the pressure of the speech community, welds the separate "red" impressions into a single, closed union of endeavor.[44]

All the more so, Weisgerber adds, does the same hold for 'higher' concepts, conceptions of the material world, and abstractions, where sensory experience assumes secondary importance.

The individual's way of perceiving and thinking about the multiplicity of phenomena, both sensory and nonsensory, is, then, determined by the finite number of categories which is language possesses; every individual, in learning to speak a language, gradually comes into possession of a 'built in' way of looking at the world:

The individual forms his intellectual *Weltanschauung* not on the basis of an independent moulding of his own experience, but under the spell of his linguistic ancestors' experiences, which have been deposited in the concepts of his language.[45]

We have now come to the crucial point in Weisgerber's theory.

[43] Weisgerber (1926), 248.
[44] *Ibid.*, 247-48.
[45] *Ibid.*, 250.

Since the points around which concepts crystallize "comprise an element of arbitrary action", it follows that in every language only *one* of many possible ways is realized; each language effects a different "conceptual partition (*Aufteilung*) of the world". Thus, Weisgerber, in reviving Humboldt's original premise that each language contains a peculiar *Weltanschauung*, defines linguistic *Weltanschauung* to mean the manner in which a language analyzes and synthesizes the 'flux of consciousness'. Weisgerber claimed that an inquiry into the conceptual world of a language constitutes an important part of the investigation of its INNER FORM. He emphasized, however, that Humboldt interpreted the term in a semiotic AND a morphological-syntactical sense; while the conceptual partition of the world differs in every language, the forms into which these concepts are ordered in each language are themselves characteristic of a particular way of thought:

Language furnishes us not only with names and concepts, that is with words, but also with forms in which we arrange these in the flux of thought. Even though the separate contents of thought are individual, there are only relatively few syntactical schemata in which they can unfold. The investigation of the processes which take place on the so-called road from thinking to speaking shows us that these sentence-schemata are not simply forms which serve man in the expression of his thoughts, but that these forms are at the same time the means which make possible and shape the unfolding of thought. Thus, here as there, our understanding is under the spell of the language which it utilizes.[46]

Weisgerber emphasizes that one can only become aware of the conceptual structure of one's native language by making differential comparisons with the conceptual structures of other languages. One method of procedure is to compare the manner in which individual languages partition a field of phenomena which is felt as belonging together. Variations show up most clearly when qualitatively different sensations belonging to the same sensory field are categorized. Returning to color designations he observes that comparatively few languages subsume color sensations under a small number of abstract color terms such as are

46   *Ibid.*, 251.

found in German. The concrete attitude of the aphasiac or normal person toward color terms can thus be taken as descriptive of a whole language. Weisgerber illustrates his thesis by pointing to the mode of color designation in several languages, from which we quote the Lithuanian and Ancient Greek examples; the quotations reveal at the same time Weisgerber's belief that some present-day language are evolutionarily more advanced than others:

Of the modern Indo-European languages it is well-known that the Lithuanians, in many respects the most conservative Indo-Europeans, have not even today arrived at general designations for all colors. Where we for example apply the designation "grey" to objects of all sorts, and apply the slight modifications "light" and "dark grey" to all shades of grey, Lithuanian possesses in place of our "grey" four or five simple words, each with a definite area of application; pìlkas (applied to wool and geese), szirmas (applied to horses), szemas (applied to horned cattle), źilas (applied to the hair of man and cattle, except horned cattle). . . . The Greek system of color designation is so different from ours that we can scarcely render unequivocally one of the many Greek color terms with one of our own. For this reason, it has seriously been contended that the Greeks were color blind, evidence of how difficult it is for us to free ourselves from the way our native language causes us to look at things. We must naturally in this case try to determine according to what principles of order the Greek language is behaving, whether we are not dealing with another division of the spectrum, whether perhaps in the southern sun not the quality but the brightness was singled out, or whether, what appears most probable to me, we are not dealing with strong after-effects of the ancient concrete mode of designation. We may thus assume that the Indo-European stood face to face with the motliness of the color world exactly as our amnesic patient: the task of classifying colors would have been just as incomprehensible to him. If we perform the same task easily, we do so only because our language offers us conceptual categories, because we possess the principles of order in the words of our language, which make possible for us a conceptual mastery.[47]

Letting the above remarks stand as a general introduction to Weisgerber's theory, we turn now to a closer examination of that theory as it appears today.

[47] *Ibid.*, 252-53.

3. WEISGERBER AND THE *WELTBILD* OF VOCABULARY

Although the problem of the relation of language to cognition is a major preoccupation of Weisgerber's and runs through all of his work, the main bulk of his theoretical writings on the subject together with the largest collection of concrete linguistic data he adduced to support his hypothesis is contained in two of his works: *Muttersprache und Geistesbildung* and *Vom Weltbild der deutschen Sprache*.[1] Weisgerber asserts that cognition results from the interaction between man's outer and inner worlds. Man's outer world is his physicial environment, relative to his position on earth. His inner world is his biological and psychological make-up, relative to that of other living organisms. The meeting place of these two realms constitutes what Weisgerber calls a "spiritual-intellectual mediary world" (*geistige Zwischenwelt*), wherein we can expect to find reflections of the other two realms: what man cognizes will obviously be dependent on his physical surroundings, and his psychophysical predispositions are reflected in his threefold role as a member of *homo sapiens*, as a member of a specific society, and as an individual. Of these three roles, Weisgerber points out that the one most decisive for the development of man's cognition of and behavior toward his physical and cultural

---

[1] All references to these works will subsequently be inserted parenthetically into the text, and will be indicated as shown below: (MG) *Muttersprache und Geistesbildung* (Göttingen, 1929); (WB) *Vom Weltbild der deutschen Sprache* (Düsseldorf, 1950); (WB, I) *Vom Weltbild der deutschen Sprache*, 1. Halbband: *Die inhaltbezogene Grammatik* (2d ed. rev.; Düsseldorf, 1953); (WB, II) *Vom Weltbild der deutschen Sprache*, 2. Halbband: *Die sprachliche Erschliessung der Welt* (2d ed. rev.; Düsseldorf, 1954).

universes is his role as a member of a specific society. This means that every member gradually comes into possession of constructs established by his society and which enable him to view and behave toward experience in much the same manner as other members of his society do. These constructs are operative "wherever man is not satisfied with an immediate, instinctive reaction, but rather in some way reflects (*sich besinnt*), conceives (*auffasst*), or even judges (*urteilt*)" (WB, I, 46).

Weisgerber illustrates this thesis by means of examples taken from astronomy and astrology (WB, I, 37-45). He points to the various gestalts that different societies have read into the 'same' heavenly constellations at various times and places. These configurations are supraindividual constructs which are learned by each new member of the society, causing him to abstract and relate the same stars.

Weisgerber compares the way in which the gestalts of the constellations are viewed by different cultures with the manner in which the different languages organize reality. In both instances certain aspects of experience are abstracted, generalized, or related according to specific cultural or linguistic categories. But according to Weisgerber language is not just one among several other modes of apprehending the outer world. Following Cassirer, he makes everyday language the source of all other forms of knowledge; the special terminologies of science, law, art, religion, and so forth are all excrescences of everyday language (WB, I, 57-58). Because language intervenes between us and reality, so to speak, categorizing reality for us, Weisgerber believes that the speakers of different languages live in different 'linguistic mediary worlds' (*sprachliche Zwischenwelten*).

Weisgerber's thesis that language is the source of all knowledge follows from Herder's interpretation of the linguistic sign as Cassirer later more explicitly formulated it in his *Philosophy of Symbolic Forms*. Cassirer's influence is patently visible in the following passage:

In order for anything in this mediary world to gain form, duration, and validity it is *essential that it be "named"*; and the further the construction of the psychic mediary world progresses, the more indispensable becomes language in the full sense. [W.'s italics; WB, 17.]

Weisgerber conjectures that in a prelinguistic experience (*Erlebnis*) of the heavens, it is doubtful whether the sun or the moon in all its phases would be grasped (*gefasst*) as one and the same object from one day to the next (WB, 17).

But language does more than merely stabilize the flux of impressions for us; it is due to language that impressions have any meaning for us in the first place. "In order for a configuration to be able to play a role as *tree* in my consciousness, even when I have it bodily before my eyes, it must of course be completely incorporated in a psychic transformation, which without language would not at all be feasible" (WB, 19). Weisgerber in effect endorses the principle of *nihil est in intellectu quod non est in lingua*; language and consciousness are identified:

We do not have to go into the controversial questions of this field [that is, of linguistic signs], whether for example ultimate possibilities of a behavior are available to man without this "fetter" of sensuousness. Since at least for the field which concerns us here, that of "reflected" (*besonnene*) behavior, the *level of the conscious and considered*, the validity of this law of sign-boundness is generally conceded. It has been particularly uncontested since Herder, that human reflection and the capacity for manipulating signs are nothing short of identical. [WB, I, 73.]

Under linguistic consciousness Weisgerber includes the cognitive processes of recognition, attending, judging, and evaluating:

1. RECOGNITION, KNOWING (*erkennen, anerkennen*). To know or recognize an object and to name it, that is, place it in a certain category, are simultaneous acts. Being placed in a certain category implies a kind of 'transformation' of the object:

The very fact that I can call the object I hold in my hand only *rose*, means that I have first recognized it as *rose*; in so doing I have *psychically transformed* it from its status as a unique occurrence into a specimen placed within the limits of an overlapping order. [WB, I, 51.]

2. ATTENDING TO (*beachten*). Weisgerber believes that we are likely to be more conscious of things we have a name for:

From a profusion of herbs we will be much less securely conscious of an unnamed plant [WB, 30-31]. . . . There is in *weed* much that is unnoticed, thrown together as a "remainder". [WB, I, 53.]

Thus the manner in which different languages categorize (*ordnen, einordnen*) things does not indicate a lack of ability to perceive differences, but rather indicates a more complex cognitive distinction (left unspecified by Weisgerber). If the French word *groseille* refers to what the German words *Johannesbeere* ('currant') and *Stachelbeere* ('gooseberry') refer to "then the distinguishableness of the two is probably not canceled out, but the mental involvement (*gedankliche Umgehen*) is certainly affected" (WB, 31).

3. JUDGING (*urteilen, beurteilen*). According to Weisgerber, any judgment which one is capable of making depends on what categories are available in one's native language. For example, the fineness or grossness of one's experience of olfactory or gustatory sensations depends largely on how finely or grossly the linguistic categories of one's native language discriminate them (WB, II, 9-16; 88-94).

4. EVALUATING (*werten, bewerten*). Weisgerber uses this term to mean that language is capable of making value statements for which there are no corresponding facts in nature. Thus, to the possible objection that when we name an object *rose* we are recognizing an order which is already prefigured in nature (*roses* can after all be classed according to shape, color, odor, etc.), Weisgerber points to words like *herb, weed, fruit, vegetable, cereal,* the referents to none of which can be said to 'exist' in nature.

It is these and similar cognitive processes that, according to Weisgerber, are possible only by means of language; the naive conception of language that sees only the fastening of a phonetic tag onto a 'thing' already 'known' in the external world is false:

Whether I then "conceive" (*auffasse*) a motion as a *walking* or as a *striding* or as a *trudging*, or whether I "categorize" a piece of furniture into *chairs* or *armchairs* or *stools*, or whether I "judge" a sensation as *sweet* or as *sour* or as *bitter* – the way from objective reality to consciousness always leads through the psychic mediary world. [WB, 19.]

So far we have considered the role language plays in cognizing only natural phenomena. But this is the area where, according to Weisgerber, the influence of language on cognition is least obvious. The part played by language in the cognitive process becomes more and more evident as we pass from the world of nature to that of material culture and finally to the realm of nonsensory, spiritual-intellectual phenomena; language thus applies to every area of human experience. This leads us to regard every language as a built-in way of viewing the world:

> Thus the impression is reinforced that in all our conscious behavior a veritable mediary world is participating, through which our conceiving, our judging, our knowing and acting pass, and which is so closely bound to linguistic media that we must designate it as the world picture of a language (*Weltbild der Sprache*). [WB, 33.]

It is apparent, then, that Weisgerber considers a language's so-called "content" words, what are traditionally called nouns, verbs, adjectives, and adverbs, as the chief determinants of its 'world picture'. Although he regards the grammar of a language too as influencing the perspective of its speakers, he seems to regard vocabulary as the more decisive factor. The reason for this is not difficult to find. Weisgerber and the other Neo-Humboldtians have worked almost exclusively with comparing Indo-European languages,[2] where the grammars are very similar and where minor differences are often difficult to interpret. The full range of meanings of words in different languages, on the other hand, as is well known, almost never overlap, and thus more readily suggest cognitive differences. However, Weisgerber does recognize grammar as a constitutive factor in the way a language organizes reality, and his thoughts on this will be discussed later. We shall now examine his theory of the linguistic sign.

The world picture of a language is fashioned according to what Weisgerber calls the two structural laws of the linguistic contents (*die Aufbaugesetze der Sprachinhalte*) of a language.

[2]   A major exception is Peter Hartmann, *Einige Grundzüge des japanischen Sprachbaues* (Heidelberg, 1952), cited by Weisgerber in WB, II, 138-39; 165-67.

These two 'laws' operate simultaneously, together determining the total content of a speaker's language. They are the laws of the sign (*Zeichen*) and of the field (*Feld*).

Following Cassirer, Weisgerber points to the tremendous advantage of the artificial linguistic sign (or symbol) over the natural one in representing temporally separated objects or events as the 'same'. The less a linguistic sign resembles its referents, the better:

What natural bleating, grasped as a sign, can do in reference to a single sheep, the artificial symbol can effect on the level of the spiritual-intellectual (*Geistigen*) in a much more momentous way: even various individuals can appear the "same" when grouped under the [same] sign, and thereby be united in the mind as a unified "object". [WB, I, 87.]

The idea that referents, when subsumed under the same categorical label, are the 'same' derives from Weisgerber's theory of word constitution, which he developed in two of his early articles.[3] There he defines the word (that is, the substantive, verb and adjective-adverb) as "not a phonetic complex to which a definite psychic content or extract of objective reality is joined by association; the word is rather an indissoluble union of sound and content, constructed on the function of the symbol".[4]

Moreover, if the word represents an indivisible whole, the components of which are sound (called variously *Laut, Lautform,* or *Name*) and content (called variously *Inhalt, Begriff,* and later, more usually, *geistiger Gegenstand*), then, Weisgerber points out, it is misleading to speak of the "meaning (*Bedeutung*) of a word". We must not define meaning as though it were the property of a word but rather as a relation (*Beziehung*) obtaining between a word's sound and its content: 'Meaning' is simply a relational term, that it, it is nothing but the relation between two real facts: something 'meaning' something, and something 'meant'.[5]

---

[3] "Die Bedeutungslehre – ein Irrweg der Sprachwissenschaft?," *Germanisch-romanische Monatsschrift*, XV (1927), 161-83, and "Vorschläge zur Methode und Terminologie der Wortforschung", *Indogermanische Forschungen*, XLVI (1928), 305-25.

[4] *Ibid.* (1927), 170.

[5] *Ibid.*

According to Weisgerber the failure to recognize the relational character of meaning is the major error of traditional semantics. This oversight, he claims, is due to the erroneous assumption that meanings are 'independent psychic substances' standing outside the word, as revealed in such expressions as '*Stuhl* means 'chair' in German', 'the word has changed its meaning', 'the word 'bright' has several meanings', and the like. Furthermore, the relationship between a word's sound-complex and its content is a reciprocal one: if viewed from the name, this relationship is termed 'meaning'; if viewed from the concept, it is termed 'designation' (*Bezeichnung*). Schematically represented, then, Weisgerber's analysis of the word looks like this:

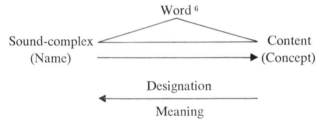

In addition to the unorthodox use of the word 'meaning' here, Weisgerber gives us no further information on the nature of the relation he is trying to show between the sound and content of a word. But as H. Kronasser has pointed out, there are only two possibilities: either the relation is realized through learning, or it is given *a priori*.[7] At any rate, Weisgerber recommends that the term 'meaning' be dispensed with and that we replace a 'science of meaning' (*Bedeutungslehre*) with a 'science of concepts' (*Begriffslehre*).

But, Weisgerber asks, how can we define linguistic concepts? He stresses the fact that a definition of the kind employed in logic and science and found also in dictionaries is misleading here, since, as Cassirer already pointed out, such a definition

[6]   See Weisgerber (1927), 182; (1928), 318; MG, 34-35.
[7]   *Handbuch der Semasiologie: Kurze Einführung in die Geschichte, Problematik und Terminologie der Bedeutungslehre* (Heidelberg, 1952), 61-62.

does no more than specify explicitly what is already prefigured in language. In other words, the criterial attributes that character- ize a concept are somehow 'present', if submerged, in the ordinary everyday usage of language. Linguistic concepts are for Weis- gerber cognitive primitives, so to speak, often not capable of being defined (that is, described in terms of other concepts) by the un- sophisticated speaker, even though the latter may be able to use them completely correctly. This is true whether color or kinship terms are concerned:

It is a well-known fact that our language [that is, German] has ac- tually assimilated all the shades of color into a rather small number of conceptual classes, and that in general there is scarcely any doubt about the distribution of the individual shades, although not a single unsophisticated speaker can logically define one of these concepts, say, *red*. Or I have no trouble specifying whether a relative of mine is my uncle or my cousin, although I would not trust myself to give a simple and adequate conceptual definition of the linguistic concept *uncle*, which I nevertheless use. This very objection, that there can be in *language* no adequately delimited concepts, is very serviceable to us, for it points out to us that it will not do to argue from the in- dividual's unconsciousness of delimitation to a lack of delimitation in the cultural property language. The fact of the matter is, rather, that the individual, whenever he employs a word concept, always surveys unconsciously the range of this concept; however, he "knows" at once whether a specific datum falls under this concept or not. Thus: I cannot, to be sure, simply specify what all the concept "uncle" in- cludes, but I can without hesitation say whether this or that relative is or is not my uncle. Thus, this concept must, again, be delimited for me. ... [MG, 56.]

Or terms for physical shapes and conditions:

Now everyone of us knows for sure what *nose* and *fog* "mean," if not in "reality," then at least in range of application, thus, ultimately in their content in accordance with the psychic mediary world. [WB, 45.]

Or 'nonsensory' phenomena:

To be able to use the word *sluggish* correctly, I must have other words at hand like *lazy, washed-out, tired, exhausted* as measuring rods. To judge a perceived person aptly as sluggish presupposes the correct use of this whole series. [WB, 32.]

Thus, being able to use a word 'correctly' (that is, in accordance with some standard of usage adopted by a speech community) and 'unconsciously' (that is, without being able to specify the criterial attributes of the word), is decisive evidence for Weisgerber that language possesses 'built-in' categories through which we apprehend reality:

A word in a language does not become my possession until I can not only pronounce it, but also *use it correctly*. In this condition of "correct usage" is *comprised basically the presence of a linguistic mediary screen*, and that becomes clear upon reflection as soon as we abolish the notion of a short circuit directly connecting the sound-complex and the outer world. [WB, I, 58.]

At any rate, to 'define' linguistic concepts Weisgerber adopts Saussure's principle of reciprocal delimitation:

A word receives its precision (*Bestimmtheit*) in language through the system to which it belongs, and so the definition must also take into account the whole system. ... If we proceed thus, the definition obtained will often be nothing more than a making conscious of the demarcations (*Abgrenzungen*) which (for us, unconscious) determine the concept in the objective structure language. [MG, 64-65.]

In describing the manner in which linguistic concepts are delimited Weisgerber points to another of their characteristics which set them off from the concepts of logic and science. Unlike the latter, which are purportedly based on 'purely intellectual criteria', linguistic concepts can be delimited by an 'affective element' (*Gefühlsmoment*) as well. This prescription is in keeping with the Humboldtian assumption, already foreshadowed in Herder, that language is a product of the total consciousness:

Because language is a cultural property in which all facets of human existence work themselves out, we find, then, intellect and feeling operative in concept formation too. But that does not justify us in dividing the concepts into two essentially different classes: some intellectually (logico-scientifically) determined, others affectively determined; and, where possible, interpreting this dichotomy as though the one kind were objectively and universally valid, and the other subjective and arbitrary. Logical concepts lead only *one* side of linguistic achievement to accessible fulfillment. [MG, 66; cf. WB, I, 92.]

The conceptual contents of words, then, are determined by their position within the synchronic conceptual systems of a language, and this position itself is delimited by both ideational and affective determinants. On this view, the phonetic configuration of a word plays no part in determining its conceptual contents. For this reason there are no such things as homonyms:

If examples like *foot* (body-part and unit of measure), *root* (part of a plant and expression in mathematics), etc., are adduced in order to prove that only "comparatively few expressions possess a single, perfectly defined and unalterably constant sense" [A. Drews, *Lehrbuch der Logik* (Berlin, 1928), p. 127], then we must point out the construction of the word (word = unification of concept and name) and emphasize that we have to do with two different words here, that find their semantic determination in two different lexical systems. [MG, 62.]

nor synonyms:

That the substantives *wave (Welle)* and *billow (Woge)* are synonymous, only the (pseudo-) logician can claim, who sees that the same object can be called *wave* or *billow*: against this we must repeat that the designation does not affect the object as such, but rather signifies (*kundgibt*) our conceptual apprehension (*begriffliche Auffassung*) of it. Whether I apprehend (*auffasse*) a unit of water as *wave* or *billow* is, indeed, conceptually something essentially different. [MG, 63.]

Instead of synonyms (different sound-complexes 'having identical meanings') and homonyms (identical sound-complexes 'having different meanings'), then, in Weisgerber's theory, we are dealing with totally different words. He believes that much of the misunderstanding about synonyms and homonyms has been conditioned by the misleading metaphor of words 'having identical or different meanings' (WB, I, 75ff.).

With Saussure's principle of reciprocal delimitation we have come to the second structural law which, in Weisgerber's theory, governs the linguistic contents of a language – the 'law of the field':

If the law of the sign enables us to understand how a linguistic sound-complex can operate as a crystallization point for a linguistic content, then the *law of the field* enables us to understand how these contents can acquire a delimitation, a precision, and thereby an applicability, even without this psychic process having to be conscious to its executors. [WB, I, 86-87.]

To illustrate the 'reality' of the law of the field, Weisgerber claims that the content of the abstract color term *grau* ('gray') in Modern German can only be fully disclosed by resorting to this law. Although the external stimuli are the same as those arrested (*festgehalten*) within those linguistic expressions that are 'thing-bound' (as in the case of the several words for gray in Lithuanian already mentioned on p. 52, he claims that *gray* cannot be satisfactorily explained purely by the stimuli:

Modern German *grau* is much less a mere response to individual impressions than a transforming intrusion of the mind into the interpretation of phenomena, and, what is more, within the framework of the total transmutation of the degrees of brilliance. But according to what principle is this intellectualized construct formed? In most dictionaries one looks in vain for a satisfactory definition of what *gray* "means." Some "natural" extract, a footing in the realm of "things" cannot be referred to. If a definition is attempted, then possibly it is in the sense that *gray* is the intermediary realm between *white* and *black*, without, however, the possibility of fixed demarcations being set from the affair. This is an important point: *gray* is actually to be understood neither as derived from "nature," nor primarily in connection with "things," as abstracted from the possible "carriers" of *gray*. It apparently owes its determination much more to an all-encompassing *linguistic* order, which is represented in the juxtaposition (*Nebeneinander*) or, better, *composition* (*Miteinander*) of the series *white-gray-black*. *Gray* is above all a value, and, what is more, not an isolated value, but a *positional value*, that derives its precision from its place within a structured whole. [WB, I, 89.]

As we have seen, the field concept of linguistics is not original with Weisgerber; it has its roots in Humboldt and especially Saussure. And although the concept is present in embryonic form in all of Weisgerber's early writings, it was only after the concept had been variously interpreted by different men and after Weisgerber had adopted a specific formulation of it, Jost Trier's, that he made systematic use of it. Before, then, investigating further the field concept as it appears in Weisgerber's total system, we shall first consider the immediate impetus which gave rise to the various field theories, and then examine Trier's particular interpretation.

4. THE 'FIELD' THEORY OF LINGUISTICS

'Field' as a linguistic term first became widely known after G. Ipsen used it in the compound 'semantic field' (*Bedeutungsfeld*) in 1924.[1] Ipsen employed the compound to characterize a group of words which are used in connection with a specific area of experience, as, for example, the Indo-European vocabulary for 'sheep' and 'sheep raising'.[2] In advancing his theory Ipsen compared a 'semantic field' to a mosaic, which later became the Humboldtians' favorite image for illustrating the manner in which experience is divided up:

This connection [of native words], however, is not to be interpreted as a stringing together on an associational thread, but rather in this way: the whole group marks off a semantic field, which is internally structured (*gegliedert*). Like in a mosaic, word is joined to word, each one shaped differently, but in such a way that the contours fit one another, and together all of them rise in a high-order sense unity, not sink into an empty abstraction.[3]

[1] Gunter Ipsen, "Der alte Orient und die Indogermanen", in *Stand und Aufgaben der Sprachwissenschaft: Festschrift für W. Streitberg* (Heidelberg, 1924), 225. 'Field' as a linguistic term had been used before Ipsen by Heinz Werner, *Die Ursprünge der Metapher* (Leipzig, 1919), 83, 111. See Hans Schwarz, "Leitmerkmale sprachlicher Felder", in *Sprache – Schlüssel zur Welt: Festschrift für Leo Weisgerber* (Düsseldorf, 1959), 245, n. 2. According to O. Ducháček, "Les champs linguistiques", *Philologica Pragensia*, III (1960), 26, the compound *Bedeutungsfeld* had been used before Ipsen by A. Stöhr in his *Lehrbuch der Logik in psychologischer Darstellung* (Leipzig, 1910). See Stephen Ullmann, *Semantics: An Introduction to the Science of Meaning* (Oxford, 1962), 244, n. 4.

[2] Cf. also Suzanne Öhman, *Wortinhalt und Weltbild, Vergleichende und methodische Studien zu Bedeutungslehre und Wortfeldtheorie* (Stockholm, 1951), 74-75, and the same author's "Theories of the 'Linguistic Field'", *Word*, IX (August, 1953), 125.

[3] Ipsen (1924).

Ipsen's term gave rise within the next several years to several rival theories of linguistic fields. Chief among these were the theories of Ipsen himself (in a revised form),[4] A. Jolles,[5] Walter Porzig,[6] and Jost Trier.[7] Of these the one that has had the most influence on later field theory (especially Weisgerber's) and is at the same time most relevant to the present study, is that of Trier. The field theories of Ipsen and Jolles will therefore not be discussed in this study.[8] Because Trier has made extensive reference to Porzig's theory in explicating his own, Porzig's theory of the linguistic field will be brought up later in connection with Trier's.

Trier has expressly acknowledged everywhere his espousal of the Humboldtian conception of language as an organism wherein all parts are conceptually related to one another, and he has enthusiastically aligned himself with the modern expression of this idea as formulated by Saussure.[9] In words reminiscent of Humboldt and Saussure, Trier defines his concept of the field as follows:

Every language is a system of selection over and against objective reality. As a matter of fact every language creates a self-sufficient and complete image of reality. ... Every language structures reality in its

[4] Ipsen, "Der neue Sprachbegriff", *Zeitschrift für Deutschkunde*, XLVI (1932), 1-18.

[5] A. Jolles, "Antike Bedeutungsfelder", *Beiträge zur Geschichte der deutschen Sprache und Literatur*, LVIII (1934), 97-109.

[6] W. Porzig, "Wesenhafte Bedeutungsbeziehungen", *ibid.*, 70-97. See also the same author's book *Das Wunder der Sprache* (2d ed. rev.; Bern, 1957), 117-35, where some of his original ideas were enlarged.

[7] Trier's major theoretical writings are: *Der deutsche Wortschatz im Sinnbezirk des Verstandes: Die Geschichte eines sprachlichen Feldes, I: Von den Anfängen bis zum Beginn des 13. Jahrhunderts* (Heidelberg, 1931), 1-26; "Sprachliche Felder", *Zeitschrift für deutsche Bildung*, VIII (1932), 417-27; "Deutsche Bedeutungsforschung", in *Germanische Philologie: Ergebnisse und Aufgaben, Festschrift für O. Behaghel* (Heidelberg, 1934), 173-200; "Das sprachliche Feld", *Neue Jahrbücher für Wissenschaft und Jugendbildung*, X (1934), 428-49.

[8] For discussions on the field theories of Ipsen and Jolles, as well as of Porzig and Jolles, see especially Öhman (1951), 72-89; (1953), 123-34; Ullmann (1957), 154-70; (1962), 243-53.

[9] Cf. especially: "In the whole of the conception [that is, his theory of the field] I feel myself indebted most strongly to Ferdinand de Saussure, and most closely akin to Leo Weisgerber." (1931), 11, n. 1.

own manner and thereby establishes the components of reality which are peculiar to this given language. The language-reality components of one language never recur in quite the same form in another, nor are they simply a straightforward copy of reality. They are instead the linguistic-conceptual realization of a view of reality proceeding from a unique but definite structuring matrix which continuously compares and contrasts, relates and distinguishes the data of reality. Implicit in the foregoing is, of course, the realization that nothing in language exists independently. Inasmuch as structuring constitutes the basic essence of language, all linguistic components are the result of structuring. The ultimate meaning of each is determined precisely and only by its relation to and function in the total linguistic structure.[10]

Trier follows Saussure too in proclaiming the word as the primary unit of language (*langue*); the sentence, of speech (*parole*). The word, then, for Trier, is the primary unit of 'sociolinguistic reality': "The questions which deal with the word are sociolinguistic questions, and he who poses them doesn't have to concern himself with the objection – made from the point of view of speech – that the word is a mere abstraction from the reality of the sentence." [11]

In Trier's theory, then, the conceptual content of every word in a language is determined by all the other words of that language. Next to and above every word (to return to the image of the mosaic) stand other words which are closely or remotely related to it conceptually. These 'conceptual relatives' taken together constitute a lexical field (*Wortfeld*) and must be distinguished from the conceptual field (*Begriffsfeld*) of which it is the outward manifestation. The latter, whose outer boundaries are coterminous with those of the lexical field, cannot be defined independently of language; only the individual words of the lexical field reveal the inner structure of the conceptual one. Moreover, there are no gaps in the lexical field; the individual words of the lexical field account for every part of the conceptual field.

According to Trier's theory, smaller lexical and conceptual fields themselves form fields of an ascending order until finally

[10]   Trier (1934), 429. Translation by H. Basilius, "Neo-Humboldtian Ethnolinguistics", *Word*, VIII (August, 1952), 100.
[11]   Trier (1931), 9.

the entire vocabulary is accounted for in an architechtonic whole. He expresses the intermediate position which the field occupies between the individual word and the entire lexicon of a language in this way:

Fields are living linguistic realities that are operative between the in-dividual words and the whole lexicon. As parts of a whole they share a characteristic feature in common with the word, in that they "articu-late" (*ergliedern sich*) [into fields of a higher order]; on the other hand, they share a common characteristic with the lexicon too, in that they "resolve" (*gliedern sich aus*) [into fields of a lower order].[12]

By postulating 'closed' conceptual fields, then, Trier provides himself with a means by which he can compare the way in which different languages, or different periods of the same language, have partitioned the 'same' area of experience. The totality of the different ways in which a language effects these divisions will then constitute that language's world picture.

To illustrate how the meaning of a word is determined by the position it occupies in its conceptual field, Trier posits the 'con-ceptual field' of PROFICIENCY RATING. He points out that, given the rating *poor*, we are unable to determine its exact meaning until we know that the exact number of members in the field are five: *excellent, good, fair, poor, very poor*; and that *poor* falls between *fair* and *very poor*.[13] Trier admits that such an example, with its strictly linear configuration, oversimplifies the field con-cept, but that the principle shown here is valid for all lexical fields: "Individual words reciprocally determine each other's meaning by their *number and position* in the total field." [14] To understand what any word means, then, Trier claims the TOTAL FIELD must be present (*gegenwärtig*) to the speaker and listener.[15] The world view of a particular speech community depends on where the 'divisions and connections' are made within the various conceptual fields.

[12]   Trier (1934), 430. Cf. also Ullmann (1957); Basilius, *loc. cit.*; Öhman (1953), 127.
[13]   Trier (1931), 6-7.
[14]   *Ibid.*
[15]   *Ibid.*, 4 and *passim*.

Instead of applying his theory of the linguistic field to different languages, Trier concentrated on comparing one field in the various synchronous stages of its history in one language. In 1931 he published the first volume of a projected study of the 'intellectual' field (*Intellektualfeld*) as it appeared in German from the beginning of the thirteenth century to the present: *Der deutsche Wortschatz im Sinnbezirk des Verstandes: Die Geschichte eines sprachlichen Feldes*.[16] Many of Trier's investigations since then have dealt with this same field. Of these investigations we shall now examine one which he himself thought pointed up the theoretical foundations of his method most clearly.[17]

Trier proposes to compare the articulation of one section of the intellectual field, the field of 'knowing facts' (*Wissen*) or 'knowing-a-thing-well' (*Sich-auf-etwas-verstehen*), as it appeared in courtly poetry around the year 1200; with the articulation of the 'same' section as it appeared a century later (1300) in the terminology of Meister Eckehart's mysticism. For the latter period Trier relies on the findings reported in the dissertation of one of his students.[18] Trier believes that by means of such a comparison he can show that "the speech community in a condition B, by virtue of its speech space knows something different (*um etwas anderes weiss*) than it knew in A, and in A knew something different than it can know in B".[19] He justifies the choice of genres to be compared on the grounds that "it compares the highest with the highest, the representative with the representative; against this, the objection that completely disparate genres and incommensurable contents are here being set side by side is countered".[20] Trier's report of his student's findings can be summarized as follows:

[16]   Cited with full bibliographical material on p. 65, n. 7.
[17]   Trier (1934), esp. 432-38.
[18]   Theophora Schneider, "Der intellektuelle Wortschatz Meister Eckeharts: Ein Beitrag zur Geschichte des deutschen Sprachinhalts" (unpublished Ph.D. dissertation, Department of Philosophy and Natural Sciences, University of Münster, 1934).
[19]   Trier (1934), 432.
[20]   *Ibid.*

In the first period, the field of intellect was organized around the series *kunst, list,* and *wîsheit.* These terms referred to very different things at that time than they do now. *Kunst* referred to the 'higher' levels of knowledge and ability; *list,* the 'lower'. What was higher or lower was determined by the social, moral, and aesthetic values of courtly culture. A *kunst* denoted any skill or discipline which society considered as reflecting or contributing toward the development of the whole person in both his mental and physical capacities, and which characterized him as a member of courtly society: how one rides, behaves toward women, how one jousts, how one treats his adversary. *Künste* also were the art of writing poetry, the liberal arts of rhetoric, music, painting, and architecture. *List* applied chiefly to technical knowledge and skills, such as astronomy, botany, mineralogy, medicine, and the crafts of the artisan, those things which were thought of as lacking the capacity to mould the whole person. On the other hand, *wîsheit,* besides being interchangeable with both *kunst* and *list* in many cases, was also used to denote their synthesis. But in this latter function *wîsheit* amounted to more than the mere sum of the meanings of *kunst* and *list*; *wîsheit* referred to man as a whole, combining intellectual, ethical, social, aesthetic, and, above all, religious elements into one concept.

The same 'field' is structured differently in Meister Eckehart a hundred years later. The 'field of knowledge' is still covered by three terms, but a different three: *wîsheit, kunst,* and *wizzen.* According to Trier, it might appear that *wizzen* has simply replaced *list,* but, he claims, such is not the case. The contents of each term have changed and so have the relations between them. *Wîsheit* no longer denotes knowledge and skill in general, but only religious or mystical wisdom. The synthesizing function of the earlier *wîsheit* is now divided between *kunst* and *wizzen,* but both terms are now devoid of all social and ethical connotations. Furthermore, the range of *kunst* is considerably narrowed by the appearance of *wizzen; kunst* now approaches the Modern German *Kunst* in applying to certain branches of knowledge. *Wizzen* signifies pure intelligence, without specifying whether this intelligence has social connotations or not. Since *list* has disappeared from the old *kunst-list* duality, and with it the socially directed conception of knowledge and skill, *wizzen* can now be made to apply to pure intelligence in anyone, regardless of how close this intelligence approaches a social ideal. To quote Trier's own words:

> The decisive thing here is that the courtly construct is so constituted that appraisal of social standing *must* be expressed in one way or another, simply through assignment to *kunst* or *list*, and that the mystical construct no longer imposes this linguistic restraint of appraising social position. It is the distinctive feature of this latter construct that the possibility is now given of speaking about a person who knows or can do something, without this necessarily having to be evaluated in language according to some social or ethical norm. [Trier's italics for *must*.][21]

Porzig had charged that Trier, in addition to not having satisfactorily explained the epistemological basis for identifying the field of intellect, has not shown any justification, even supposing that proof could be adduced for its 'presence' in Modern High German, for assuming that the same field was 'present' in Middle High German.[22] He contends that Trier's concept of the intellectual field has been derived from extralinguistic data and is therefore an arbitrary construct.

To this charge of arbitrariness Trier has answered that the difference between his and Porzig's conception of the field is really based on the difference between their conceptions of language.

> It apparently depends, whether arbitrary or not, on what all one regards as belonging to the realm of language. If one – as we ourselves do – considers the contents as part of language, the speech contents let it be noted, and not only the meanings of words, then such accretions as we have in mind are also given through language. Thus the difference between so-called linguistically given requisites and so-called formalogical connections and divisions loses the absoluteness which it necessarily has for every conception of language

[21] *Ibid.*, 437.
[22] Porzig (1934), 71.

that regards the contents *and their order* as lying outside language. [Trier's italics.] [23]

Porzig, in giving his concept of the field,[24] had claimed that there are certain 'essential semantic relationships' obtaining between verbs and nouns and between adjectives and nouns. 'To go' presupposes with 'the feet', 'to ride' presupposes in a 'vehicle', 'to grasp' presupposes with 'the hands', 'blond' presupposes 'the hair', etc.[25] Porzig believes that from such concrete 'elementary semantic fields' (*elementare Bedeutungsfelder*), where the data are 'linguistically given', more and more abstract ones are derived.

Trier claims that his fields too are linguistically given, albeit not in the single-worded and meaning-oriented way that Porzig's are. He believes, furthermore, that the total structure of a language 'speaks for itself' (*weiss zu sagen*) in assigning this or that word or word-group to a field:

> By reason of the absolute power (*Machtvollkommenheit*) that our common, present-day language exercises over us in ordering contents, we posit the field.[26]

He claims that the 'formalogical dimension' has itself been 'built into' (*ist eingegangen*) the linguistic structure and does not stand outside the linguistic domain.

We shall now proceed to examine in some detail Weisgerber's theory of how the vocabulary of German (and related languages) is constructed with regard to content, that is, how speech contents are "stamped (*ausgeprägt*), fixed (*festgelegt*), and demarcated (*umgrenzt*)" (WB, I, 120). Of course the two most active forces in this process, according to Weisgerber, derive from the operation of the laws of the sign and of the field. However, since German vocabulary consists of not only root or stem words but also derivatives and compositions, a third approach, developed from

[23]   Trier (1934), 441.
[24]   For references see p. 65, n. 6.
[25]   Porzig's reason for making a verb or adjective the nucleus of a semantic field, with an inherent subject or object as satellite, is to avoid ambiguity: one can *grasp* with the hand only, but one can do many things with the hand. Cf. Öhman (1953), 129.
[26]   Trier (1934), 441.

the other two, must be invoked to explain the relationship of derivations and compositions to the linguistic world picture. This third approach is accounted for by what Weisgerber calls the operation of 'lexical rank' (*Wortstand*). Moreover, he insists that these three approaches are kept separate only for reasons of methodological expediency; in concrete speech they work together in varying degrees.

Weisgerber begins his inquiry in the area where the linguistic sign itself might be regarded as determining its own content. This area is characterized by its close connection with things (*enge Sachgebundenheit*). As an illustration Weisgerber takes the sphere of animal cries. He observes that in German the largest number of animal cries appear as 'thing-bound' (*sachgebunden, gegenstandgebunden*), that is, they are used only in connection with the one animal whose cries they linguistically imitate: only frogs *quaken* ('croak'), only horses *wiehern* ('whinny'), only cows *muhen* ('moo'), etc. However, we must not, he insists, confuse the actual cry with its linguistic representation: "The psychic objectification which is bound up with this process does not constitute a recasting to the extent that the value of the linguistic sign directly elicited from the natural sound is abolished" (WB, I, 123-24). There are cases, then, where we can almost speak of a paralllelism of sound-complex, speech content, and reality; the content of the word appearing simply as a psychic mediation (*geistige Vermittlung*) between the sound-complex and the animal cry.

Weisgerber points out that such an analysis becomes more complicated, however, when we come to words that are used of more than one kind of animal; both dogs and foxes *bellen* ('bark'), both oxen and lions *brüllen* ('bellow', 'roar'), etc. If we try to justify such classifications by appealing to the objective world, we are beset with difficulties. Why for instance should dogs and foxes *bellen*, but wolves *heulen* ('howl'); or why does the noise made by the wings of *brummenden* ('droning') beetles appear in the same category as the voice of the *brummenden* ('grunting') bear? In cases such as these, where the same sign includes 'different' noises, we still encounter linguistic categories that are strongly determined by the world of things, but which nevertheless constitute 'condensations' (*Zusammenfassungen*), a kind of 'psychic grasping together' (*geistigen Zusammengriff*).

Finally, when we come to consider bird cries, such as *zwitschern* ('twitter'), we can no longer rely for a definition of its content on the simple relation: sound-complex/thing; the content of *zwitschern* is determined primarily by its position in a field which includes several other bird cries: "Which birds *zwitschern* cannot be established by appealing to the realm of things alone, but only by knowing that it is also important for the German language that birds *trillern* ('warble'), *flöten* ('whistle'), *etc.*" (WB, I, 125).

Even though the 'psychic coherence' is somewhat loose, according to Weisgerber the whole range of animal cries can nevertheless be regarded as constituting a lexical field in itself. While many of the substructures of the field, like that of *wiehern,* can be grasped from their 'pure relation to things', without their connection with their field neighbors being clearly perceptible; other substructures, like that of *zwitschern*, depend chiefly on the operation of the 'law of the field' for their validity.

However, because of its limited applicability Weisgerber assigns a modest role to the more simple forms of the sign function in determining speech content. Of far greater importance in this respect is the operation of the law of the field. To show how the majority of speech content must be understood as articulating (*ergliedern*) from the whole field to which it belongs, he examines the field of color in Modern German. Although even in this field there are terms which he regards as 'thing-bound' (in ascending levels of abstraction: *kornblumenartig* ['like the corn-flower'], *kornblumenblau* ['corn-flower blue'], and finally *blond* ['blond'], which is 'thing-bound' to the extent that it is only used of the color of hair), he claims that such terms assume secondary importance when compared with the 'imposing intellectual performance which our abstract color terms achieve'. He contends that the thing-bound conceptualizations found in some languages, such as Lithuanian, have no abstract counterparts to those found, say, in Modern German. The color blue in German, for example, can only be defined according to its position in the total color field.[27] To the possible objection that *blue* might only be a 'plural concept', that is, that it might merely comprise the SUM of all shades of blue, each of which is somehow conceived prior to language, Weisgerber answers: "To possess the German word *blau* it is not a necessary prerequiste that we have previously experienced all shades of *blue* sensorily, and subsumed them mentally under one term; therefore, such a subsumption cannot be the deciding factor for the German word content either" (WB, I, 129). We are left, so Weisgerber maintains, only with the assumption that a structural principle supervenes which delimits the domain of all possible shades of *blue* from the totality of all other color shades, and which causes us to conceive these variations as the 'same'. This structural principle, he claims, is a reflection of the operation of a linguistic field.

However, whereas Trier illustrated his concept of the field by showing how the word *good* has a different value according to whether it occurs in a series of four, five, or six members, Weisgerber maintains that such a simplified concept of the linguistic field applies to only a part of language. In addition to these SERIAL STRUCTURES Weisgerber proposes that language contains more elaborate constructs which he calls SURFACE and DEPTH STRUCTURES. Furthermore, besides these SINGLE-LAYERED fields, that is, fields whose structure 'appears to be governed by a unified points of view', there are *multilayered* fields, where several viewpoints seem to be operating. We shall now consider some examples of these different types of fields.

Weisgerber believes that the best example of a serial structure within a single-layered field is the one of numerical seriality. Rejecting the idea of an abstract 'linguistic-numerical field' which is the same for all languages, he cites several passages from Cassirer's *Philosophy of Symbolic Forms* which he claims supports his thesis of "how much our thinking in the realm of numbers has to do with the mediary world of our native language" (WB, I, 135). One such passage is:

[27]   For the example of *gray,* see p. 63, above.

Among the Bushmen the numbers, strictly speaking, extend only to two: the term for three means only "many" and is used, in conjunction with finger language, for all numbers up to ten. ... The Binandele language of New Guinea has only the numerals one, two and three, while numbers above three must be expressed by circumlocutions.[28]

Weisgerber concludes from this datum:

But it is clear that these expansions are very limited, and they are, above all in the sense of the psychic mediary world, not the same as simple numbers; $2 + 3$ may be mathematically the "same" as 5, but for the psychic process (*geistiges Verfahren*) it is not the same whether we deal with a sum or a totality. ... [WB, I, 135-36.][29]

According to Weisgerber (and Cassirer), then, circumlocution (*Umschreibung*) evokes a cognition different from that which the single word does.

Weisgerber's thesis that there is no universal cognition of number appears to be conditioned mainly by his belief in the 'progressive' theory of language, which the data collected by Cassirer seemed to corroborate. Those languages whose specifications of number are 'tied' to things in the real world represent a more 'primitive' stage of development. Thus, the connection between numerical seriality and the linguistic mediary world becomes even clearer, according to Weisgerber, when we see "how slowly the pure, abstract number world is loosened from its confinement to the world of the senses". From the fact that certain tribes of New Guinea count in a sequence that runs from the fingers of the left hand to the wrist, the elbow, the shoulder, the left side of the neck, the left breast, the chest, the right breast, the right side of the neck, etc.,[30] Weisgerber concludes that since counting gestures are here necessary components of counting, "apparently something mentally (*gedanklich*) quite different is involved than purely abstract work with counting-words and ciphers".

[28]   Cassirer (1953), 243; quoted by Weisgerber in WB, I, 135.
[29]   In the first edition of *WB* Weisgerber had written "thinking" (*Denken*), p. 67, instead of "psychic process".
[30]   Cassirer (1953), 230.

A mental syncretism like that existing between number and gesture is also found between number and the thing counted, whereby "a definite quantity and a definite thing coalesce (*verschmelzen*) into a mental kind of unity" (WB, I, 137). As an illustration of this phenomenon he cites Cassirer's example taken from the language of the Fiji Islands, where different words are used to designate groups of different objects, such as coconuts, canoes, fish, etc.[31] Vestiges of this mental syncretism, Weisgerber maintains, can be found in Modern German and English: *Stiege* ('score') and *Mandel* ('sitting') are applied to eggs and sheaves; *Groschen* and *Karat* to coins and weights, etc.

An example of a SURFACE STRUCTURE within a single-layered field is provided, according to Weisgerber, by the kinship terminology of Modern German. Here, all terms are ordered essentially according to the single principle of generational sequence (terms to distinguish relatives on the paternal, maternal, or spousal side, etc., no longer playing a part), and fan out to form a two-dimensional structure. As an example of a SOLID STRUCTURE within a single-layered field, Weisgerber adduces the image of the color solid (WB, I, 132).

Weisgerber illustrates a MULTILAYERED field, one that functions from more than one angle, by the field having to do with the EXPIRATION OF LIFE. He claims that this field is trilayered and can be pictorially represented as a series of three concentric circles. In the innermost ring human dying (*sterben*) is set off from the dying of animals (*verenden*) and of plants (*eingehen*). In the two outer rings the whole field of dying is apprehended from two points of view: the center ring is the objective locus and thus stresses the actual circumstances accompanying death; the outer ring is the subjective locus and thus sets the affective attitude towards death in relief.

Another example of a multilayered field in Modern German adduced by Weisgerber is that of the field of 'use', the kernel of which is structured by the three terms *verwenden* (applied to objects found in nature which man uses for his own purposes:

[31]   Cassirer (1953), 233.

wood for burning, water for washing, etc.), *gebrauchen* (applied to objects which are manufactured for specific purposes: soap, brushes, etc.), and *benutzen* (applied to objects of an impersonal or public nature: streets, public vehicles, etc.). Weisgerber regards as evidence for the demarcation of this 'field' the fact that English can employ the one term 'use' for all three German words (WB, I, 146).

Similarly, Weisgerber attempts to isolate the multilayered field of 'taking place' by employing distributional data found in German alone. He suggests that, because the generic term *stattfinden* ('to take place') can be substituted intransitively in all the environments where specific terms, such as *abhalten, veranstalten,* etc., are used, this is evidence for the presence of a unified 'field'. Paradigmatically represented:

eine Versammlung		sie wird abgehalten:	thus abhalten
ein Wettspiel		es wird veranstaltet:	thus veranstalten
ein Vortrag		er wird gehalten:	thus halten
eine Ausstellung	findet statt	sie wird veranstaltet:	thus veranstalten
eine Reise		sie wird unternommen:	thus unternehmen
eine Eröffnung		sie wird vorgenommen:	thus vornehmen
ein Prozess		er wird (durch)geführt:	thus (durch)führen

Up to this point Weisgerber has dealt only with root or stem words, with which he claimed the laws of the sign and the field were adequate to cope. To show how words displaying affixation fit into his system he adopts the two concepts of lexical niche (*Wortnische*) and lexical rank (*Wortstand*). The former term goes back to K. Baldinger's idea of a 'semantic niche',[32] and as used by Weisgerber the term refers to a group of words defined formally by their having in common a derivational affix (whether uniform or not) and contentually by their referring to the same area of 'things'. The latter term was borrowed from H. L. Stoltenberg[33] and is used by Weisgerber to refer to a group of words defined formally the same as the lexical niche is, but semantically it is defined according to what Weisgerber calls a "closed semantic performance" (WB, I, 162).

[32] K. Baldinger, *Kollektivsuffixe und Kollektivbegriff* (Berlin, 1950).
[33] H. L. Stoltenberg, *Neue Sprachgestaltung* (Lahr, 1930).

Weisgerber attempts to show the difference between these two concepts by examining the combinatory tendencies of one of Modern German's most productive suffixes, -ling. He claims that most of the words formed with this suffix can be arranged in various lexical niches: *Pflegling* ('foster-child'), *Säugling* ('suckling'), *Lehrling* ('apprentice'), *Sprechling* ('one beginning to speak'), etc., where the common semantic denominator NECESSITY OF CARE can be posited; *Dümmling* ('block-head'), *Weichling* ('molly-coddle'), *Neuling* ('novice'), *Fremdling* (stranger'), etc. Though Weisgerber concedes that connections between these groups can be vaguely perceived, he claims that not much of a 'mental unity' is apparent when we pass from one group to the other; in spite of formally identical markers, we seem to be dealing with groups of varying content. But the mistake here, Weisgerber maintains, is that we have taken OBJECTIVE content as the chief criterion for inclusion in a lexical grouping (and hence in many cases it is the root and not the suffix that determines the membership), and not LINGUISTIC content, which transcends the objective world; just as formal criteria alone should not determine the 'function' of a word, neither should the world of 'things'. If, then, we survey all these groups together, a common denominator does emerge which places all of the words ending in -ling into one lexical RANK. This denominator is the idea of a person being in an UNFINISHED or INCOMPLETE state, and it is this ingredient that he suggests is conceptually present when we use a word ending in -ling.

All three determinants, then, sign-designation, field structure, and lexical rank, contribute, each in its own way, to the full unfolding (*Entfaltung, Fächerung*) of linguistic fields. To illustrate how all three interact within a linguistic field, Weisgerber continues with the example of the color field. Positing as the basic series of this field the common color adjectives, he makes each of these adjectives the center of a word-family (*Wortsippe*), "which clusters around the adjective and stands in a livingly felt connection with it" (WB, I, 176). These word-families may consist of substantives and abstract nouns (*das Rot, die Röte*), adjectival derivatives (*rötlich*), verbal formations (*röten, erröten*), all of which "apparently act very closely together in the mental disclosure and elaboration of the color world" (WB, I, 176).

The other example by which Weisgerber chooses to illustrate the complete unfolding of a field is that of the field of *Verstoss* ('offense'). He claims that the field is controlled by two coordinates: the degree of responsibility (that is, to what extent the doer is involved with respect to knowledge, will, and natural inclination) and the norms which are offended against (whether custom, law, morality, etc.). He finds each coordinate to be composed of seven units so that the resulting field comprises forty-nine members (WB, I, 181ff.).

Before proceeding to Weisgerber's theory of grammar and syntax, we shall first examine the manner in which he believes his concept of the lexical field applies to man's total universe. As mentioned earlier he divides this universe into three areas: nature, material culture, and the spiritual-intellectual sphere; the potential of language to transform the real world becoming more apparent as we progress from one area to the next in the order mentioned. But in apperception and conceptualization within all three realms, Weisgerber acknowledges the fact that man's physical and cultural conditions will be reflected in his vocabulary. This is true of course whether we consider languages or dialects: "That a Low Saxon coastal dialect displays everywhere a characteristic stamp as compared with an Alemannic Alpine dialect is the necessary consequence of the *diversity of environments, occupations, predominant interests, starting points of images and analogies,* etc." (WB, II, 41).

To illustrate how nature is 'transformed' by the power of language to "stamp pregiven things and phenomena into the objects of consciousness (WB, II, 95), Weisgerber cites the following passage from Karl Vossler:

It is already possible to read our predominant interests out of our vocabulary. In the tropics there are Negro languages which have 50 to 60 names for various kinds of palm trees but no generic term for palm tree. These Negroes live from the fruit of palm trees and have very precise vegetarian interests but lack botanical ones. The gauchos of the Argentine had about 200 expressions for the colors of horses but only four plant names: *pasto, paja, careos, yuyos; pasto* was the name for all cattle fodder, *paja* for every variety of straw (for bedding down animals), *cardo* for all ligniform vegetation, *yuyos* for the remaining vegetable kingdom, lilies and roses, herbs, and cabbage. Thus whatever the interest of the moment, it fixes itself like an aimed gun upon definite things and finds its thrusts in the vocabulary.[34]

From such data as this, Weisgerber concludes that the function of language, once linguistic categories are established, is to perpetuate the cognitive perspective which they create:

Objective reality and human interests meet in linguistic impress (*Prägung*). A picture of the plant world so completely tuned to the needs of cattle breeding becomes "real" within these linguistic resources and makes this picture obligatory for this sphere of life. [WB, II, 80.]

Weisgerber recognizes, then, that the initial motivation toward the formation of linguistic categories is supplied by environmental or cultural needs. Thus, in Middle High German the zoological world was divided into four categories, according to mode of locomotion: *visch* (everything that swims), *vogel* (everything that flies), *wurm* (everything that crawls), and *tier* (everything that runs, and thus not corresponding to Modern German *Tier*, the generic term for animal). At Luther's time we find the same categories except that now a new category is added, *viehe*, which includes domestic animals, and thus cuts across some of the other categories. But we still find no generic term for animal because "the need for a more inclusive concept . . . has not yet asserted itself" (WB, II, 80). It was not until the eighteenth century that the generic term *Tier* appeared; at the same time the individual zoological orders themselves underwent a transformation, due especially to Linné's six classes of the quadrupeds, fowl, amphibians, fish, insects, and worms. The 'creation' of these categories gave rise in turn to new cognitive tendencies: "The most important period is the eighteenth century with the 'discovery' of the

---

[34] Karl Vossler, "Volksprachen und Weltsprachen", *Welt und Wort* (1946), 98; translation by Basilius, 101.

insect world, through which attention was not only directed at
hitherto unnoticed species, but even the categories of birds and
worms received renewed attention" (WB, II, 80).

Weisgerber claims that even in that division of nature where
we might expect a close correspondence in vocabulary from
language to language, the area of the inorganic and enduring
phenomena of the universe and landscape, such as mountains,
valleys, rivers, forests, etc., we find evidence that the same things
are cognized differently in different languages. In support of this
thesis Weisgerber cites the work of P. Zinsli, especially the latter's
book *Ground and Ridge: The Mountain World in the Mirror of
the Swiss-German Alpine Dialects*.[35]

By comparing the manner in which the speakers of certain
Swiss dialects designate features of their surroundings with the
manner in which the Standard German-speaking tourists designate these same features, Zinsli concludes that the mountain
dweller 'sees' his world differently than the tourist does. This is
to be expected, he says, for the difference stems from the nature
of their respective interests: where the mountain dweller may see
only forbidding heights and barren mountain areas which make
it difficult for him to make a living, these same features may
inspire the tourist, who is not preoccupied with such matters, to
phantasy and adventure. What may be left unnamed or scarcely
mentioned by the Alp dweller, is imaginatively depicted by the
mountain-climbing tourist: "Every height becomes a *peak* or
crescent, a *tooth* or even a *needle*." [36] Even differences in grammatical gender are utilized: "*Der Bernina* is then known more
expressively as the feminine peak *die Bernina*." [37]

According to Zinsli the two most apparent images that emerge
from examining the various terms for mountain formations are
those of the image of the 'mountain monster' (*Bergungetüm*),
which anatomical terms like *head, horn, back, nose, tongue,* etc.,

---

[35]   *Grund und Grad: Die Bergwelt im Spiegel der schweizer-deutschen
Alpenmundarten* (Bern [1946]).
[36]   Zinsli, 244.
[37]   *Ibid.*

seem to suggest, and the image of the 'mountain edifice' (*Berg-gebäu*), which architectural terms like *ridge, roof, tower, gate, wall,* etc., imply;[38] the terms from both images taken together are classified by Zinsli into nine basic types, called 'fields' by Weisgerber, according to their geometrical forms. Weisgerber recognizes that in every instance nothing of the content that was originally projected in these terms may still be 'perceived' (*ge-spürt*), but that the total structural orientation certainly is not without significance: "... much may re-echo of what has moved men's thoughts when they mastered and interpreted the richness of natural forms with linguistic comprehension" (WB, II, 71).

According to Weisgerber the further we progress from in-organic nature the more decisive language becomes in its role as shaper of the data of the outer world. Even time and space are not entirely free from the formative influence of language. Evidence of differences in the cognition of time, Weisgerber claims, can be seen from the various ways in which languages and dialects divide the year. In addition to the Standard German names for the seasons, Swiss German possesses 'thing-bound' designations, such as *Blüe(j)et, Laubris, Dürbruch,* etc., which Weisgerber glosses respectively as 'period of blooming', 'time of leaf falling', and 'time of snow thawing'. He concludes that examples like these and similar ones (*three paternosters long*) taken from German dialects show "how little the abstract concepts of time are indigenous there and how instead concrete and familiar events intervene with its duration" (WB, II, 73).

To illustrate the part that language plays in our cognition of space, Weisgerber, in addition to pointing to 'thing-bound' spatial designations abounding in German (and English), such as *span, acre, fathom,* etc., refers to a problem that more probably belongs in the sphere of logic than of 'nature' – Zeno's paradox of the race between Achilles and the tortoise. Weisgerber contends that at the base of the paradox lay the failure of Homeric Greek to distinguish between the concepts of a definite course to be covered in common by the two rivals, a *Strecke,* and the specific path,

[38]   *Ibid.,* 209-24.

Weg, that each rival in fact covers on this common course. Achilles can never overtake the tortoise because the 'race' is being run not on a neutral *Strecke*, but in accordance with each of the rivals' *Wege*; consequently, the rivals never meet, for their *Wege* are never the same (WB, II, 75-78).

However, according to Weisgerber "the area where the ordering and conceptual capacity of the linguistic process is most apparent" (WB, II, 78) is the world of organic nature. To this area belong terms for vegetation which the various languages employ and which were discussed earlier. But he claims the most illuminating observations can be made within that division of nature "where the natural conditions of man himself are linguistically disclosed" (WB, II, 81). This area includes the linguistic conceptualization of kinship relationships, body parts, and sensory phenomena.

Weisgerber claims that beyond the basic kinship relationships covered in English by the terms father, mother, husband, wife, son, and daughter, which he believes probably have exact correspondences the world over (WB, II, 81),[39] all other kinship designations represent cognitive SYNTHESES of the primitive terms. For example German *Onkel* (and English *uncle*) expresses the relationships 'father's brother', 'mother's brother', 'father's sister's husband', 'mother's sister's husband'. But in Latin there is no kinship term that covers all these, and only these, relationships; Latin *patruus* for example covers only the relationship 'father's brother'. Weisgerber concludes that:

... it obviously makes a difference whether the same brother of my father becomes *Onkel*, in accordance with Modern German usage, or whether he becomes *patruus*, in accordance with Latin usage: this is not a case of a mere difference in naming, but rather a difference in "intellectualized objects" (*geistigen Gegenstände*). ... If we had both lived in ancient Rome, he could never have become *Onkel* mentally: as *patruus* he would have been transformed also intellectually (*geistig*),

[39] However, some writers doubt whether these are absolutely universal human concepts. See for example Anthony F. C. Wallace and John Atkins, "The Meaning of Kinship Terms", *American Anthropologist*, LXII (February, 1960), 76.

but in a different way, into the "compressed" (*verdichteten*) father-brother, in accordance with the organizing principle of the Latin language. [WB, I, 65.]

As evidence that body parts are conceived (*vorgestellt*) differently, sometimes even within the same language, Weisgerber draws attention to the fact that in certain situations the North German says. "You're stepping on my *Bein* [usually glossed in English as 'leg']," whereas the South and West German, instead of *Bein*, usually says *Fuss* ('foot'); moreover, he points out that it is usually the toes (*Zehen*) that are actually trod upon. He concludes that although the distinction between *Fuss* and *Bein* can be made by all speakers of German, the distinction is "apparently not generally prescribed, and that we are able to conceive relationships that are absolutely linguistic, and in which [the distinction] is not brought out in the same way and to the same degree" (WB, I, 110). Evidence from other languages, he believes, shows that here too the human body is 'divided differently': In Russian, *ruka* generally means both 'arm' and 'hand'; *noga*, both 'leg' and 'foot'; *palec*, both 'fingers' and 'toes'; however Russian can make these distinctions if necessary. Similarly, the many 'synonyms' for 'head', 'mouth', 'nose', etc., in the German (and other) dialects also indicate different conceptions of body parts.

But it is linguistic designation of sensory phenomena that Weisgerber believes provides the most convincing evidence for linguistic relativity. Returning to the field of color, he claims that the color words in the various languages are not simple reflections of relationships existing in nature; thus they cannot be explained in purely physical or physiological terms:

Between reality and consciousness a transformative process must also be interpolated here. More correctly: we have to reckon here with *two processes* that lead from the physical via the physiological to the conscious, whereby in consciousness itself the individual-psychic impression must be separated from its linguistic-conceptual recoinage. [WB, II, 84.]

Weisgerber claims that one of the most convincing demonstrations of the power of language to transform sensory phenomena into constructs of its own making derives from the color controversy prior to 1900:

It [the controversy] arose from the difficulty encountered in translating the color words of the early Greeks, especially Homer. One gets into unexpected difficulties in trying to find the precise synonyms, for example, for Gr. *dzanthós, glaukós, ōchrós* and others of the commonest color words. In the one case *yellow* or *green* fits, in the next it doesn't. If one considers all occurrences together, one arrives at amazing conclusions such as this: *ōchrós* sometimes has the meaning of *greenish yellow*, sometimes the meaning *red; chlōrós* means *yellowish green* on occasion, but also *grayish brown*, etc. One has attempted to translate all of these words with *brilliant* on the assumption that the Greeks were less interested in the particular hue or tint than in the intensity (luster quality), particularly under the light conditions of the southern sky. This explanation was abortive, however, since Greek also has a well developed sequence of luster adjectives *lamprós, phaidrós, aigléeís*, etc. The other alternative was to assume that this translation problem offered evidence for the study of the development of the color sense in the human race. From this point of view several observers seriously maintained that in our terms the Greeks must have been collectively color blind. But this conclusion also failed to hold water and thus the way remained open for the correct solution: If the observed discrepancies were attributable neither to the nature of the phenomena themselves nor to the structure of the human eye, then they must be grounded in the conceptual midway lying between reality and expression, that is, in the manner of human judgment. [WB, II, 85-86.] [40]

What is true for the cognition of colors is, so Weisgerber contends, fundamentally valid for the senses of taste and smell. It cannot be demonstrated, he points out, that definite basic kinds of gustatory or olfactory sensations are derivable from chemical or physiological facts alone. If, granting that *sour* or *fragrant* are chiefly facts of consciousness, we turn to psychology to tell us something, we are met with the following discovery: we can only learn how these sensations penetrate man's consciousness from the report he himself gives us; and since this report must necessarily be given in his native language, his cognition of these im-

[40]   Translation by Basilius, 102.

pressions will to a large extent be predetermined for him by the categories his language makes available to him. Weisgerber claims that in Standard German (and other Indo-European languages) gustatory and olfactory sensations are perceived 'abstractly' or 'concretely', depending on the nature of the linguistic category: of the everyday words referring to taste, three of them, *sauer* ('sour'), *süss* ('sweet'), and *bitter* ('bitter'), are 'abstract', that is, the sources that cause us to designate a sensation by any one of these terms can be various, and thus the sources "do not appear to be bound with any of [them]" (WB, II, 91-92), whereas the only source for judging a sensation as pure *salzig* ('salty') is that of cooking salt. On the other hand, of the common words referring to smell, apart from a few like *duftig* ('fragrant') and *stinkig* ('stinking'), most are 'thing-bound' in varying degrees: *modrig* ('moldy'), *würzig* ('spicy'), *blumig* ('flowery'), *harzig* ('resinous'), etc.

According to Weisgerber, language plays a fundamentally different role in the second area of man's universe, the domain of material culture. Here we are not interpreting pregiven data which exist 'independently' of man, but rather objects that have been created by him. We might then expect a complete correspondence here between things and linguistic fields. But this correspondence may occur only in the mind of the manufacturer, not in that of the user. Those who coin technical terms have such correspondences in mind, but to the user of products, who is a representative of the general consciousness, that is, a speaker of the everyday language, these products "appear in the full richness of human judgment and appraisal" (WB, II, 97). If, for example, we consider the lexical field of 'receptacle' (*Behälter*) in German, we find the words *Kiste, Kanne, Krug, Sack, Büchse, Dose, Tube, Ballon, Fass, Gefäss,* and many others which can be ordered according to material, size, form, purpose, etc. The latter, however, are not the only, nor the most important, cognitive determinants:

... to such distinctions based on the pure order of products is added much that the *autonomy of the linguistic mediary world* causes us to recognize (*erkennen lässt*). What is the difference between *Gefäss* and *Behälter*? Size alone doesn't determine it . . . ; nor does purpose . . . ; certainly not then "objectivity" alone. Nevertheless an inner connection between *Gefäss*, content, and possessor suggests itself: a *Gefäss* for domestic use (also of more careful manufacture) and its appropriate content complement one another just as for the more impersonal *Behälter* even the content is more irrelevant. These inner connections are not purely "objective," but rather they are established by man. [WB, II, 99.]

For examples of the way the field approach applies to the spiritual-intellectual sphere, Weisgerber explores the fields of human behavior and intellect. His discussion of the latter field relies on Trier's investigations which were discussed earlier. We shall now turn to Weisgerber's theory of how the grammar of a language influences the 'world picture' of its speakers.

5. WEISGERBER'S THEORY OF GRAMMAR AND THE *WELTBILD*

In discussing the epistemological status of the three word classes of substantive, verb, and adjective, Weisgerber claims that each class represents a different mode of cognition. Thus in Modern High German, color phenomena appear as adjectives (*farbig, bunt, rot, grünlich,* etc.), but luster is expressed by verbs (*glänzen, leuchten, funkeln, glitzern,* etc.) and by adjectivals derived from verbs (*glänzend, blinkend,* etc.)[1] We may, then, according to Weisgerber, speak here of an adjectival conception of reality whereby colors are regarded as static attributes of an object, and of a verbal view whereby bodies EMANATE their luster. This conclusion, he claims, is corroborated rather than refuted when we consider the 'derived' verbs *blauen, grünen,* and *grauen.* Both the fact that there are lacunae in this verbal series (*roten*, weissen**) and the fact that the distribution of the attested forms is limited (only the sky 'blues', plants 'green', and the day 'grays') indicate to Weisgerber that this perspective is unusual for speakers of German:

It is remote from our thoughts (*es liegt uns fern*) to bring the color sensation into an active relationship with the colored object; the latter is for us distinctly the *bearer* of color and not the *transmitter* of it. And only the strength and depth out of which the sky generates its *blue,* and the plant its *green,* causes a verb to appear here that char-

---

[1] Without attempting to explain the reasons for it, Weisgerber notes that in the older Germanic languages these relations were reversed: colors were expressed as verbs, lusters as adjectives (WB, II, 132-33); for a fuller discussion of this phenomenon see his earlier article "Adjektivische und verbale Auffassung der Gesichtsempfindungen",, *Wörter und Sachen,* XII (1929), 197-226. Cf. also Basilius, 103.

acterizes the permanent state as a stirring of life, as a form of expression in accordance with its being. [WB, II, 130-31.]

On the basis of considering the examples above, Weisgerber points out that we might, in spite of his thesis that reality is 'transformed' in the individual word, be led to assume that there is nevertheless a correspondence between reality and the word classes: the substantivized plant words are constructed on 'things' 'in' the outer world; the sensory adjectives go back to 'attributes' of things. That this assumption is unjustified, however, becomes clear, he believes, as soon as we begin to investigate the characteristic ways in which language classifies the data of the external world for the consciousness. At this point Weisgerber invokes the concept of hypostatization as it has been recently developed by E. Leisi in his book *Word Content: Its Structure in German and English*.[2] There Leisi defines hypostatization as the tendency of language

to reify ... every phenomenon of any sort, in so far as it can be designated by *one* word, and to endow it with an existence independent of, and detached from, other phenomena, that is, [a tendency] to elevate it to an accidentless substance. ... Thus, language forces us more or less to perceive (*erblicken*) in *journey, hip, family, billow* an independent, detached "object," in *green, empty, close* an independent, detached "quality," in *stand, wait, begin* a detached, independent "activity," etc.[3]

Weisgerber believes that Leisi, though he makes no claim that language is a 'linguistic disclosure of the world', nevertheless, by employing his own characteristic methods, reaches conclusions similar to those of Weisgerber. It would, therefore, seem advisable to examine Leisi's theory more closely.

Leisi, because he compares language with usage, calls his theory of language sociological; each individual word is like a social custom (*Brauch*): its content is defined by the conditions

---

[2] *Der Wortinhalt: Seine Struktur im Deutschen und Englischen* (2d ed. rev.; Heidelberg, 1961). For other references to language and hypostatization see p. 24, n. 2, of Leisi's book.
[3] Leisi, 24.

(*Bedingungen*) governing its use.[4] Leisi notes that "when a person uses a word correctly, this means that the condtions which govern the use of the word are 'known' to him. However, that does not mean at all that he knows them consciously and could name them in detail." [5] Proceeding from Jespersen's assertion that 'triangle' and 'three-sided rectilinear figure' 'mean' the same thing,[6] Leisi concedes that 'purely logically' they do, but that nevertheless a difference in view (*Anschauung*) is suggested by the two designations:

If I speak of a "triangle," then the thing is represented – in the terminology of the Scholastics – as a *substance* without accidents, that is, as a representative of the category "triangles"; nothing is said about its attributes. On the other hand, if I speak of a "three-sided rectilinear figure," then the thing is conceived (*aufgefasst*) as a substance (figure) with two individual characteristics (rectilinear, three-sided).[7]

If, for example, considering only substantives for the moment, we try to determine how much 'substance' is actually present in the outer world and how much is postulated by language, we find that, excluding abstract substantives, the clearest examples of hypostatization are substantives designating events, qualities, and relations: *journey, flight, weather, lightning, cough, quarrel, sale, sleep, death, mumps, nearness, neighborhood,* etc. Moreover, in so far as the substantive refers to 'things', there are types of substantives of varying degrees of 'objectivity'; Leisi calls these types individuatives (*Individuativa*), collectives (*Kollektiva*), partitives (*Partitiva*), and privatives (*Privativa*).

The first of these groups, the individuatives, corresponds most closely to the 'objective' world and is characterized as denoting "an object (or organism) which is isolated and dependent to the extent that it cannot be taken from the place where it is situated to another place without injury, nor, as the name implies, can it

4   *Ibid.,* 13ff.
5   *Ibid.,* 23.
6   Otto Jespersen, *The Philosophy of Grammar* (New York, 1924), 93.
7   Leisi, 23.

be divided without destruction or damage".[8] Examples are *person, key, apple,* all animal names, *book, cloud,* etc. This group of words is itself 'conditional' in various ways: in the case of *apple* and *book* a definite substance as well as a definite form are conditions for the word; with *cube* and *ring* only form is a condition; with *a glass, an iron* only substance enters as a condition. But between these two subclasses comes one in which neither form nor substance is clearly determinative, "but which is still not completely free".[9] To this subclass belong words like German *Klumpen, Klotz, Scholle, Brocken,* and English *lump, clod, clot, sheet,* etc. Words of this type are characterized by rarely having exact equivalents in other languages, and by being difficult to translate and learn. Comparing German *Klumpen* with English *lump,* Leisi notes that the conditions of form and substance correspond only partly: both words are used to refer to *clay, dough, butter, iron,* and *lead*; in addition, however, German *Klumpen* is used in reference to *gold* and *blood,* where English uses *nugget* and *clot*; and where English *lump* applies to *coal* and *sugar,* German uses *Brocken* and *Stück.* Leisi concludes that for the areas where *Klumpen* and *lump* do not overlap in their application, *Klumpen* still covers the denominators of wetness and plasticity, *lump* the denominators of dryness and brittleness.

Leisi divides collectives into group collectives (substantives which denote a plurality of individuals: *family, company, team,* etc.), generic collectives (substantives which, when used in the singular, denote not a group of individuals, but the whole class: *game, fowl, cattle, police, furniture,* etc.), and mass words. His definition of the latter is taken from Jespersen: ". . . words which do not call up the idea of some definite thing with a certain shape or precise limits",[10] and include *sand, iron, water, air, foam,* etc. Leisi points out that such words here too are likely to have no exact correspondences in other languages. The closest English counterparts of German *Brei,* for example, are all limited by

8   *Ibid.,* 26.
9   *Ibid.,* 27.
10   Jespersen, 98.

material or other conditions: *porridge* (oats), *mud* (earth), *paste* (consistency), *pap* (purpose: for children or sick people), etc.

The category of partitives includes substantives that denote an objectively 'dependent part' of an object or organism. Leisi notes that here too, as in all 'thing-words', we find the tendency to regard the denotation as an independent whole. Instances of this category include *cheek, hip, peak, corner, leg, mountain*, etc.

The category of privatives is defined by Leisi as including words denoting an absence of substance: *hole, crack, tunnel, wound*, etc.

In like manner Leisi tries to show how his concept of conditions applies to adjectives and verbs. Adjectival content, for example, can be determined by static qualities (*white*), dynamic qualities (*fast*), a relationship between the designated object and something else (*close, frequent, naked*) actuality and potentiality (English *ill* is only actual, *invalid* only potential; German *krank* is both), etc. Verbs are also treated as hypostatizations of various conditions: of action (*fall, beckon, burn*, etc.), of state (*sit, hang, squat*, etc.). Privative verbs show the condition that 'something is happening contrary to the normal or expected' (*lack, wait, remain*, etc.).

Leisi, then, attempts to show systematically that the traditional notions of the substantive being coordinate with a 'thing', the verb with an 'activity', and the adjective with a 'quality', are true to a limited extent only, and that each word class is actually composed of a variety of semantic correlates. Although Weisgerber agrees with Leisi and praises him for taking a 'sociological' approach and thereby avoiding the pitfalls of a 'psychological' one, he nevertheless asks: Is there not SOME semantic correlate common to all members of a word class in a language? Turning to H. Brinkmann's analysis of the German verb, Weisgerber notes that Brinkmann, far from finding a common 'primary function' of the German verb, identifies FIVE grammatical types, each with its own semantic correlate.[11] Thus, however difficult it may

[11]   See H. Brinkmann, "Die Wortarten im Deutschen", *Wirkendes Wort*, I (1950), 65-79.

be to discover a semantic correlate covering ALL grammatical types of the German verb, Weisgerber insists that at least the various types become clearly distinguished when we compare other languages, especially those totally unrelated to German. Thus, German *see* is an 'action' word, but in Japanese it appears as an 'event'. Weisgerber quotes P. Hartmann with approval, leaving the question open whether we can even call the Japanese form a 'verb' or not; the passage also sets in relief the inadequacy of the translation method alone in 'proving' linguistic relativity:

A *wa ga sakura wo miru* "my cherry-blossom-seeing" betrays by its very translation [!?] that it is not as active as a "I see the cherry blossoms"; for in *wo miru* there is a seeing-ability. The seeing refers to cherry blossoms present in the environment; the seeing has an antipole, a point of reference in the cherry blossoms because it finds in them a place for perception. This point of reference is for the Japanese not as it is for us, the terminal point of an activity, but rather the place where something may happen. For even seeing is for the Japanese an event and not an action which is bound with a subject and which grasps a thing. Seeing takes place in the subject, but arises first through a reference which it has in the environment, in the perceiving subject. Perception results from a referring to the object, not from the will of the subject.[12]

But in spite of the difficulty of "making conscious the actual achievement (*Leistung*) of the individual word classes" (WB, II, 140), Weisgerber nevertheless feels that they do predispose us to think in a certain direction. The fact that no common semantic 'substratum' can be shown to run through the various types of, say, the substantive (thing names, material names, abstract names, etc.) does not invalidate the notion of a common 'function' of the substantive: "It doesn't depend on the extent to which we can show a corresponding uniformity in 'things,' but rather *whether the 'reality' of the word class is in itself acting in the same direction,* and whether consequently the modes of shaping experience, which are held together by the same word class, pos-

---

[12] P. Hartmann, *Einige Grundzüge des japanischen Sprachbaues* (Heidelberg, 1952), 91. Hartmann himself calls the Japanese 'verb' a nominal form, 70.

sess a common root in their achievement of it" (W.'s italics; WB, II, 140-41).

According to Weisgerber, a language's major word classes are structures intermediate between its vocabulary and its sentence structure. Following Saussure and Trier he recognizes the sentence as the primary unit of speech (*parole*). There are, according to Weisgerber, three factors which secure the structural and conceptual unity of sentences, and which make their temporal lineality comprehensible as simultaneous wholes: sentence intonation, congruity, and encompassment (*Umklammerung*). Of these Weisgerber considers sentence intonation to be the most obvious sensory index of sentence unity. However, he believes congruity and parenthesis express more characteristically the integral unity of German sentences.

Congruity (that is, formal agreement among certain sentence components in regard to person, gender, number, case, etc.), in contrast to the 'isolating' languages, appears well developed in the Indo-European group. In addition to regarding the morphemes which express congruity as indicators of thought unity within the sentence, Weisgerber holds that they facilitate the ready expression of thought itself (WB, II, 186). Moreover, in discussing the grammatical category of gender in German, Weisgerber implies that languages not having this feature lack a certain ease of expression; he thus tacitly assumes the existence of some sort of absolute scale by which we can measure such matters:

... even though the original meaning of gender distinction is almost lost, agreement between nouns, adjectives, and pronouns according to grammatical gender remains a very important means for the construction of our sentences, for the flexibilities of German word order, for the continuation of a sequence of thought from one sentence to another. A comparison with the capabilities of languages behaving otherwise is very instructive for realizing the effect of these characteristics. [WB, I, 79.]

Of the three factors, however, Weisgerber believes that the one that most clearly shows the 'simultaneity of succession' in the German sentence is the 'law of encompassment' (*Gesetz der Um-*

klammerung). This 'law', which was first explicitly formulated by E. Drach and which he calls a cardinal principle of German syntax,[13] refers to the well-known syntactic pattern in German whereby conceptual contents that 'belong together' are incapsulated within a single phrase or construction, the terminal lexemes thus forming a kind of conceptual boundary. Drach intended this law to apply to almost any type of construction, as the following examples of his show:

article + substantive   der (gute) Wein.
auxiliary verb + nominal form er ist (schnell) gekommen.
verb + object   wir holen (morgen) Brot.

Weisgerber believes that much can be learned about cognition from examining sentences found in scientific and formal German exemplifying this principle. He asks us to consider the following sentence (matching numbers indicate 'immediate constituents'):

(Translation: 'They arrived after an unusually great delay which was caused by a storm that had suddenly burst forth during the previous night.') Weisgerber claims that such a sentence shows that "the thought must be surveyed in its principal features and structured in its full development, before the filling in of the sentence scheme can begin" (WB, II, 192). He points out that another version of this sentence (one that is more likely to occur in everyday German) might be: *Sie kamen an, wenn sie auch eine Verspätung hatten, die ungewöhnlich gross war, weil ein uner-*

[13] *Grundgedanken der deutschen Satzlehre* (Frankfurt am Main, 1937).

warteter Sturm sie aufgehalten hatte, der plötzlich losgebrochen war, etc. From his commentary on this version, one gathers that the 'encompassing' principle is more conducive to disciplined thinking:

> But anyone can see that not only are external limits set for this process, but that the slightest deviation can give another direction to the whole: it's the freedom of improvisation, however, at the same time the arbitrariness of sequence, the choice of emphasis, the contingency of fixing. This freedom appears essentially limited by the law of encompassment. Individual characteristics cannot be taken up under the influence of the moment and then be dropped again; they must try to exhaust the breadth of a situation. The attention cannot wander or roam around at will either, so that what has gone before is lost sight of: the parentheses standing open demand that they be closed at the right place. Above all, the sequence of thoughts cannot be broken off at any place whatsoever, but must be led to a conclusion in accordance with its inner consistency. [WB, II, 193-94.]

In contrast to German, Weisgerber points out that encompassment plays a much smaller role in French. Instead, he compares the formation of the components in a typical French sentence to the removal of pearls from a string. He illustrates this characteristic with the following French sentence (the slashes are Weisgerber's): *les verbes radicaux subsistent / en grand nombre, / et avec de nombreuses particularités / singulières, / propres à chaque verbe* (Meillet). Compared to the German 'equivalent' (*Die Wurzelverben sind [in grosser Zahl <und mit vielen (auffälligen « jedem Verb eigentümlichen ») Besonderheiten>] erhalten*), he believes the 'loose' construction of the components in the French sentence indicates that the thought does not have to be grasped in its entirety before the sentence begins: "the beginning, the middle [of the French sentence] need to take comparatively little notice of the continuation and the end" (WB, II, 191).

Weisgerber believes that every language contains a small number of basic sentence types (*Satzbaupläne*) from which all concrete sentences of the languages are generated, and which predispose the speakers to think in certain ways. While praising the contributions made by E. Drach and H. Glinz in their analysis of

German sentence structure (WB, I, 245-50; WB, II, 170-76),[14] Weisgerber feels that neither writer is sufficiently concerned with finding primitive sentence models, nor does he believe that either writer stresses adequately the peculiar relationship obtaining between the sentence structure of different languages and their speakers' cognition of reality.

The most important contribution in this direction, Weisgerber believes, is that offered by H. Brinkmann.[15] Weisgerber accepts Brinkmann's thesis that all simple declarative sentences in Modern German are derived from one of the two basic types: subject + intransitive verb (*die Rose blüht,* 'the rose blooms'), which Brinkmann calls an 'event sentence' (*Vorgangssatz*); and subject + transitive verb + object (*der Vater schloss die Tür,* 'father closed the door'), which he calls an 'action sentence' (*Handlungssatz*). Neither one of these sentence types, Brinkmann insists (and Weisgerber follows him), can be derived from the other.

To show how these two sentence types contain built-in ways of viewing reality, Weisgerber again invokes the concept of hypostatization. He claims that the many sentences of the type, subject + intransitive verb, where the subject is an animate being, such as *die Sträucher grünen* ('the shrubs are turning green') and *die Kinder wandern* ('the children are hiking'), and where we can in some sense speak of an actor performing an action, have caused us to "generalize a thought pattern" and "ordinarily attribute to the subject a stronger psychic position (in the sense of participation or even causation)" than is "objectively" justified in most cases (WB, II, 199). For instance, in what sense can we speak of an 'active doer' in sentences having inanimate subjects, such as *der Wagen fährt* ('the car is running'), *das Schiff sinkt* ('the ship is sinking'), *der Balken bricht* ('the beam is breaking')?

---

[14] In addition to Drach's book see Hans Glinz, *Die innere Form des Deutschen* (2d ed. rev.; Bern, 1961). For a summary of Drach's book see H. A. Basilius, "A Structuralist View of German Syntax", *Modern Language Journal*, XXXVI (1953), 130-34. For a review of Glinz's book see W. G. Moulton in *Language*, XXIX (1953), 175-80.

[15] "Der deutsche Satz als sprachliche Gestalt", *Wirkendes Wort*, 1. Sonderheft (1952), 12-26.

The same is true for the other basic sentence type containing subject, transitive verb, and object. The many concrete instances of this type have caused the speakers of German (and other Indo-European languages by implication) to 'see activity' (*Grundsehweise der Tätigkeit*) in all sentences containing these components, regarding the subject as the source, and the object as the target of action. However, Weisgerber points out, there are infinite cases where such an interpretation cannot be maintained: *die Kinder singen ein Lied* ('the children are singing a song'), *die Blumen zieren den Garten* ('flowers adorn the garden'), *die Leute glauben eine Nachricht* ('the people believe a piece of news'), *die Nebel füllen das Tal* ('fog is filling the valley') (WB, II, 200).[16]

Weisgerber claims that from comparing the lexical and grammatical structures of different languages we can, with some justification, speak of a language's relative 'tendencies' to organize or view experience in a certain way. He notes that these tendencies have often been expressed in the form of opposing pairs: concrete (*anschaulich*) – abstract, static-dynamic, synthetic-analytic. In comparing French with German,[17] Weisgerber claims that, in general, German is 'concrete' compared to the more

---

[16]   Whorf makes the same point in contrasting English, as a representative of 'Standard Average European', with Hopi: "Our normal sentence, unless imperative, must have some substantive before its verb, a requirement that corresponds to the philosophical and also naive notion of an actor who produces an action. This last might not have been so if English had had thousands of verbs like 'hold', denoting positions. But most of our verbs follow a type of segmentation that isolates from nature what we call 'actions', that is, moving outlines. Following majority rule, we therefore read action into every sentence, even into 'I hold it'. A moment's reflection will show that 'hold' is no action but a state of relative positions. Yet we think of it and even see it as an action because language formulates it in the same way as it formulates more numerous expressions, like 'I strike it', which deal with movements and changes." *Language, Thought, and Reality: Selected Writings of Benjamin Lee Whorf*, ed. John B. Carroll (Cambridge, Mass., 1956), 242-43. Weisgerber in fact later quotes this same passage when discussing Whorf (WB, II, 266-67).

[17]   Weisgerber chooses to compare French with German because "as a closely related language it [French] is similar to German, and as a Romance language it is nevertheless far enough away to be grasped in its individuality" (WB, II, 212-13).

'abstract' tendency of French and the other Romance languages, and that this contrast is most apparent in the greater tendency of German to form compound nouns, and of French to use derivational suffixes. He points out that there are thousands of compound nouns in German where place, form, or activity is highly specified: *Schlafraum* ('dormitory'), *Hörsaal* ('*auditorium*'), *Schlachthaus* ('slaughterhouse'), *Schwimmplatz* ('swimming site'), *Brutkasten* ('breeding-cage'), *Waschhaus* ('wash-house'), *Tintenfass* ('inkwell'), *Aschenbecher* ('ash tray'), *Kohlenbrenner* ('charcoal burner'), *Kesselschmied* ('copersmith'), *Bürstenbinder* ('brush-maker'), *Seifensieder* ('soap-boiler'), etc. When we compare these words with their French counterparts, we find: *dortoir, auditoire, abbatoir, nageoir, nichoir, lavoir, encrier, charbonnier, chaudronnier, brossier, savonnier,* etc., where the concept of the 'primary' morpheme is probably the 'same' but the 'concreteness' of place, form, and activity appears as a uniform and abstract *-oir, -ier*.

Weisgerber concedes that there are cases (like *Aschenbecher*) which the German may not conceive 'vividly' (*anschaulich*) ("all the more so since it is quite often no *Becher* ["beaker"?] at all"), but that the productivity of this type of word-composition justifies us in regarding it as "something important for the language" (WB, II, 214). He describes what different cognitive experiences he believes composition and suffixal derivation evoke:

Composition can look into the particularity of the individual instance; it can depict, emphasize, make vivid. Derivation, on the other hand, sees series of events and phenomena under a unified viewpoint. The uniform *-ier* is the general reference to the professional relation to an object; this alone is emphasized without it being intended or possible to go into the individual characteristics of the particular instance. In this respect there is contained in every single one of these word pairs, *Kohlenbrenner: charbonnier, Schlafsaal: dortoir,* a gradation of concreteness; and though this gradation may not appear as essential in the individual instance, it is multiplied in the profusion of cases. And it can on the whole be said that in the vision of the German language large parts of the world appear more motley, more graphic, more concrete, where in the vision of the French language the recurrent rather than the individual features are presented more easily. The mode of uniform derivation is one remote from life, and is on that

account certainly a more comprehensive form of grasping. The motley sequence of compounds likes to linger in immediate happening
and can thereby come in danger of overlooking the differences between the essential and the unessential, the constant and the accidental. [WB, II, 214-15.]

Weisgerber observes that the preference of German for the specific is evident elsewhere in the vocabulary. If we examine the
lexical fields of REST and MOVEMENT we note the greater multiplicity of terms that German has at its disposal in these areas as
compared with French. Where German usually designates sta-
tionary location by *stehen, sitzen, liegen, hangen,* French uses
only *être* except when necessary, then it has available *être debout,
être assis, être couché.* The same is true for verbs of motion. In
situations where German usually employs *gehen, reiten, fahren,
radeln,* etc., French uses the generic *aller.* German is much more
specific too about kind and direction of activity than French: *il
est tombé: er ist hin-(um-, herab-, hinaus-,* etc.)*gefallen* (WB, II,
216).

In taking up the STATIC-DYNAMIC duality, Weisgerber refers to
C. Bally's well-known designation of French and German respectively by these terms. Bally defines the static mode as one which
"is satisfied to characterize things with a label so to speak, and
to present events as ready-made happenings".[18] According to
Weisgerber, the dynamic mode, on the other hand, "describes
and defines things, representing events in their development, in
their becoming" (WB, II, 222).

Weisgerber regards as evidence that German is more "dynamic' than French the more frequent use of verbs in German
specifying exact kinds of activity and change. Corresponding to
the already mentioned comparison of German *stehen, liegen,
sitzen, hangen,* with the 'more colorless' French *être,* are the
transitive counterparts *stellen, legen, setzen, hängen,* which represent a 'still greater closeness to reality' than the uniform French
mettre: "How strongly here the peculiarity of the event is placed

---

[18] Charles Bally, *Linguistique générale et linguistique française* (Paris,
1932), 369.

in the foreground, is shown when the uniform French *mettre* is compared with German's necessity of following the concrete event into its individual characteristics: *einen Hut aufsetzen* ('to put on a hat'), *ein Kleid anziehen* ('to put on a dress'), *eine Schürze umbinden* ('to put on an apron'), etc." (WB, II, 222).

Another feature indicating the 'dynamic' character of German is, according to Weisgerber, its well-developed role of aspect as compared to French. Aspect, according to Weisgerber, is revealed not only in the verbal forms themselves, in which respect French is potentially superior to German in that it has three past tenses: *imparfait, passé défini,* and *passé composé* (even though the *passé défini* has limited applications), but is also disclosed through other linguistic resources where, he believes, German displays a 'conspicuous richness'. One such resource is the simple German verb: "... it is impossible to compare, with the clarity, simplicity, and verbal force of French, anything of the variety with which the generation and evocation of phenomena can be extracted from the simplest German verbs" (WB, II, 223). Thus, from the presence of several 'simple' verbs in German having to do with snow: *schneien* ('to snow'), *verschneien* ('to snow up'), *zuschneien* ('to snow to'), *beschneien* ('to cover with snow'), *anschneien* ('to snow on'), *überschneien* ('to snow over'), etc., Weisgerber argues that none of the languages closely related to German approach German in the 'forcefulness' (*Eindringlichkeit*) with which it presents in this respect "a condition under the most diverse circumstances and with manifold effect". Characteristically German, according to Weisgerber, is also the possibility of "synthesizing very impressively (*eindrucksstark*) behavior and effect in a single verb": *auspfeifen* ('to boo') an actor, *wegdenken* ('to think away') something, *vertrinken* ('to drink away') one's money, etc. (WB, II, 223).

But still more indicative for Weisgerber of the dynamic character of German is the fact that "the inner connections of phenomena are seen" even in word and sentence formation. He refers to Bally's belief that compounds in German, like *Wanduhr* ('wall clock') and *Handschuh* ('glove', lit. 'hand-shoe'), are evidence of something dynamic insofar as they show the result of an action: 'the clock which has been hung on the wall', etc. Although Weisgerber concedes that Bally "may perhaps be projecting into many of these observations more than is ordinarily vivid to the linguistic consciousness", he still believes that the general structural tendency toward compound formation is itself evidence of German's proclivity to indicate "the origin or effect of an object" (WB, II, 224). Other structural principles in German that indicate 'dynamism' are: the distinctions between prepositions that occur with the dative and accusative, where a state can be regarded as the result of an action; the preference for expressions with *es*, which shows an "immersion into becoming and happening" (WB, II, 225); the preference for the substantivized infinitive with its 'verbal' character.

Going to the third duality, synthetic-analytic, Weisgerber observes that "all [!] modern languages are to be characterized as analytic, compared with, say, Latin" (WB, II, 226), but that they are analytic in varying degrees. German for example is more conservative than French or English in preserving inflectional endings (*des Hauses: de la maison*). The term 'synthetic' can also be applied to compound formations, which appear well developed in German. From the various types of compounds in German, such as *Filzhut* ('felt hat'), *Dummkopf* ('blockhead'), *Vergissmeinnicht* ('forget-me-not'), *loskaufen* ('ransom'), *argwöhnen* ('suspect'), *wahrsagen* ('prophesy'), Weisgerber concludes: "How much a synthetic process like this works itself out in the impression of one's thoughts can be observed in any attempt at translation, whether it be from individual compounds or from sentences where these compounds abound" (WB, II, 227).

6. SUMMARY AND APPRAISAL

We shall now attempt a critical evaluation of the Neo-Humboldt-ian proposition that every language determines the 'world picture' of its speakers. Under language the Humboldtians are primarily concerned with vocabulary, word classes, and sentence forma-tion, but since most of the work done by the Humboldtians has dealt with the comparison of Indo-European languages, whose grammatical structures are closely similar to one another, it is the vocabulary items – the free forms of nouns, verbs, and adjec-tives – that the Humboldtians believe reflect the most apparent differences among the 'world pictures' of the speakers of these languages.

Weisgerber, the leading spokesman of the Neo-Humboldtians, claims that the 'value' or 'content' of linguistic units is deter-mined by the operation of two 'laws', those of the linguistic 'sign' and the 'field'. Since it is the latter 'law' which, according to the Humboldtians, operates differently in every language and which accounts for the chief differences in the world pictures of lan-guages, we shall begin with a discussion of the concept of the 'field' as it applies to the vocabulary of a language.

Trier and Weisgerber claim everywhere that each word in a language has a precise 'value', and that that 'value' is determined by the position it occupies in the 'field' to which it 'belongs'. These 'fields' are somehow 'present' to us when we speak and think, and they are 'present' to the auditor if he is to understand us. The question immediately arises, however: How much of the vocabulary of a language are we to take into account? For obvi-ously no one can be said to possess the whole of his language's vocabulary.[1] As we saw, Weisgerber's only restriction here is that we consider only words that are "representative of the general consciousness".[2] However, this raises another question: How can we objectively determine which words belong to the 'general consciousness'? Even if we agreed to consider words that occur with a certain frequency as belonging to the 'general consciousness', would not the fact that no two individuals possess, either passively or actively, identical total vocabularies, and yet are usually able to communicate reasonably well with one another, mean that even the words they possessed in common would not have the same 'values' for each speaker?

The foregoing observations, it would appear, are enough to disprove the field theorists' thesis that every word in a language has the same 'value' for all its speakers. The most that might be maintained at this point is that each speaker possesses his own 'field', made available by his language. But what about the principle of reciprocal delimitation itself? Trier compares his lexical fields to the scale of grading used in school examination reports (*excellent, good,* etc.).[3] But is this a valid comparison? As Trier himself admits, the analogy is artificial, for it depends on a secondary or derivative use made of some words, the meanings of which are not usually so clearly demarcated in everyday linguistic usage. Nevertheless Trier claims, and Weisgerber follows him, that the principle that each word derives its full 'value' from the number and position of the other words in its 'field' is equally valid for all 'normal fields' in the language. But where are these 'normal fields'?

Beginning with Weisgerber's divisions of 'nature' and 'material culture', there is no cogent reason for assuming that, because terms denoting colors, body parts, kinship relationships, man-made products, and so forth refer to objectively demarcated sectors of experience, speakers, in using a term that applies to one

[1]   Cf. Schwarz, 246-47; N. C. W. Spence, "Linguistic Fields, Conceptual Systems and the *Weltbild*", *Transactions of the Philological Society* (1961), 93-94.
[2]   See p. 86, above.
[3]   See p. 67, above.

of these sectors, are necessarily aware of that term's alleged 'positional value' within the whole sector. However, if there is at least some objective basis in experience for the isolation of such 'fields', what evidence is there for the isolation of Weisgerber's and Trier's more abstract 'fields'? Weisgerber seems to regard as evidence for the unity of the 'field of use'[4] in Modern German the fact that the generic term 'use' in English can be used in places where German must employ one of several specific terms, according to the object being used. But why should the fact that one language has a word of higher-level abstraction for expressing phenomena where another language has only specific terms for expressing the same phenomena be taken as evidence for the existence of a unified 'field' in the second language?

Realizing this perhaps, Weisgerber has attempted to demarcate the 'field of taking place'[5] in Modern German by employing distributional criteria found in German alone. But this approach is inadequate for the following reasons. In the first place, from Weisgerber's paradigm alone there is nothing to demand that the verbs *abhalten, veranstalten,* etc., be transformed substitutes of the generic term *stattfinden*; we could after all replace *stattfinden* in every case with other verbs, such as *beginnen, enden,* etc., which Weisgerber would presumably not want to consider as semantic 'equivalents' for *stattfinden.* Secondly, even supposing that only the verb *stattfinden* could be transformationally sub-stituted in all the linguistic environments that the terms *abhalten, veranstalten,* etc., occur in, and only in those environments, this would mean that only those 'fields' in a language that happened to have a generic (single-word?) term broad enough to substitute for every (single-word?) term which Weisgerber intuitively feels as constituting a 'field', could be empirically isolated.

For the isolation of other fields, especially Trier's highly ab-stract 'fields of intellect', there is simply the investigator's own intuition to guide him. Trier's fields are, as Porzig rightly says, 'logically' determined and are not given by the linguistic data

4   See p. 76, above.
5   See p. 77, above.

itself. In describing the Humboldtians' method, Waterman writes:

Any evaluation of Neo-Humboldtian thinking must distinguish sharply between theory and practice. To the extent that they have applied their theories they use the methods and techniques of philology, depending, for instance, upon introspection and *Sprachgefühl* to determine the boundaries of a given field. Trier's monograph on the various meanings of the concept "intellect" in Middle High German affords an excellent illustration. He simply combs the literature of the period for general references, lets the context determine the narrower meaning of a term, then by careful comparison subjectively determines the respective boundaries of the various lexical items; the resulting pattern he calls a field.[6]

There is of course nothing unusual about the use of *Sprachgefühl* in linguistic analysis. As Lees says: "It is precisely this *Sprachgefühl*, this intuitive notion about linguistic structure, which, together with the sentences of a language, forms the empirical basis of grammatical analysis," but, he adds, "it is precisely the purpose of linguistic science to render explicit and rigorous whatever is vague about these intuitive feelings."[7] However, neither Trier nor anyone else has shown how we might isolate a 'field' of synonyms, whether we regard the existence of true synonyms as a fiction or not. To quote Lees again:

Recognizing that, if meaning were explained in terms of a person's total social and psychological response to expressions, there would probably be no true synonyms, some have suggested that grammatical analysis must be based upon some notion of DEGREE of semantic similarity. No one, however, has yet shown how meanings might be quantified or how in practice a degree of synonymy could be used to isolate grammatical units.[8]

If, then, in the absence of distributional criteria for determining the membership of a 'field', we are left to the intuition of the individual investigator, we might expect no two investigators ever to agree on the exact number of lexical items to be included in a given 'field'.

[6]   John T. Waterman, "Benjamin Lee Whorf and Linguistic Field-Theory", *Southwestern Journal of Anthropology*, XIII (Autumn, 1957), 209-10.
[7]   Robert B. Lees, Review of *Syntactic Structures* by Noam Chomsky, *Language*, XXXIII, No. 3 (1957), 399, n. 40.
[8]   *Ibid.*, 398; cf. 395.

But apart from the question of whether linguistic 'fields' actually 'exist', what evidence can empirical science offer in support of the Humboldtian contention that words represent hypostatizations of fixed 'values' at all? Trier himself has admitted that the terms *kunst* and *list* were used interchangeably sometimes,[9] and that words can overlap in their fields.[10] Scheidweiler too has pointed out that sometimes even the same author used the same word with completely different meanings.[11] But apart from such concessions and 'discrepancies' concerning the 'values' of specific words, can it be argued IN PRINCIPLE that words have constant 'values' or meanings? Are not words, when actively used, always found embedded in a context, both verbal and nonverbal, and is it not the context in which words occur that gives words the meaning they have in the first place? Words standing alone have no meaning or, more precisely, they have no single meaning.[12] Moreover, since the meaning of a total utterance cannot be derived from an inspection of the individual words comprising the utterance, how can we ascribe to words so much as a 'core' of 'value' or meaning that is constant from one context to another?[13] Indeed, why call words the units of meaning at all? As Lenneberg says:

From the proposition that language and knowledge constitute an entity it need not follow that individual words correspond to specific "units" of knowledge. ... There is no cogent reason to assume that the grammarian's articulation of the stream of speech is coterminous with an articulation of knowledge or the intellect.[14]

⁹   Trier (1931), 150.
¹⁰   *Ibid.*, 90; (1934), 448.
¹¹   F. Scheidweiler, "Die Wortfeldtheorie", *Zeitschrift für deutsches Altertum*, LXXIX (1942), 264. Cf. also Spence, 95.
¹²   Cf. George A. Miller, *Language and Communication* (New York, 1951), 112.
¹³   Cf. J. R. Firth, who rejects "words as isolates corresponding to concepts or ideas, often endeavoring to combine a constant core with a field of indeterminacy". Firth, "Report" in *Proceedings of the Seventh International Congress of Linguists* (London, 1956), 5.
¹⁴   Eric H. Lenneberg, "A Note on Cassirer's Philosophy of Language", *Philosophy and Phenomenological Research*, XV, No. 4 (1955), 517. In pointing out the arbitrariness of calling isolated words the units of mean-

Moreover, as we saw, Weisgerber, in his excessive preoccupation with individual words, was led to the belief that speakers are conscious of no more and no less than the general meanings of morphemes.[15] But, Lenneberg objects:

It seems more fruitful to assume [This assertion and the following are based on evidence from experimental psychology. See George Humphrey, *Thinking: An Introduction to Experimental Psychology*, chs. 4 and 8 (London, 1951); Miller, *Language and Communication, passim.*] that much more is cognized than is expressed by individual morphemes. Morphemes and their meaning are regarded more appropriately as mnemotechnical pegs of a whole situation which is brought into consciousness by the statement as a whole. The general meaning of morphemes is probably of lesser importance in cognition than the SUM OF ASSOCIATIONS bound up with the complete utterance, or even with individual morphemes or groups of morphemes.[16]

Longacre has pointed out that, when we consider context, variations in the usage of individual words are to a certain extent insignificant:

There is, in fact, an amazing suppleness in language for describing the "fullness of reality," and this suppleness is to a large degree due to the shaping and reshaping of vocabulary items to particular contexts. The fineness and adequacy of the items-in-particular-contexts as a descriptive calculus is such that there is probably a sense in which divergencies in the vocabulary grids themselves are ultimately irrelevant. The abstraction and hypostatizing of the "vocabulary grids" may be the fundamental fallacy.[17]

Once it is recognized that words are not embodiments of invariant meanings, then much of the evidence brought forward by

---

ing, Miller has suggested the possibility of drawing up a dictionary using some other verbal unit, for example the syllable, instead of the word; *Language and Communication*, 112.

[15] See p. 55, above.

[16] Lenneberg (1953), 466.

[17] Robert E. Longacre, Review of *Language and Reality* by Wilbur M. Urban and *Four Articles on Metalinguistics* by Benjamin Lee Whorf, *Language*, XXXII, No. 2 (1956), 302. Longacre quotes Urban to show that the latter, in contrast to Whorf, recognized the central importance of context: "This is what we mean by saying that the meaning of a word does not exist apart from its context" (111) and "Every meaning, we have seen, presupposes some systematic context" (195).

Weisgerber to show that the speakers of different languages cognize differently is questionable. The mere fact for example that language A employs a generic term to express what language B uses several different terms to express,[18] or that the range of application of a word in language A probably never coincides completely with that of a word in language B [19] cannot itself be taken as evidence that, in responding verbally to the same situation, a speaker of language A experiences anything significantly different from what a speaker of language B experiences.

More obvious in this connection is the fact that no valid conclusions can be drawn concerning differences in cognition from examining the individual morphemes of social formulas. For example, to show that body parts are cognized differently in different languages and dialects, Weisgerber cites the fact that a North German usually says "You're stepping on my leg (*Bein*)" to a South German's "You're stepping on my foot (*Fuss*)".[20] But it is difficult to imagine here that either speaker 'has in mind' the literal meaning of *Bein* or *Fuss*. Rather, each speaker's total utterance should be regarded as a response to an unpleasant physical situation, both of which, total verbal response and stimulus situation, have been associatively linked in the past.[21]

But nowhere are conclusions regarding the meanings of individual words more precarious than when Weisgerber tries to attach cognitive significance to the metaphors found in a language.[22] Weisgerber fails to recognize the fact that it is the very nature of language to be metaphorical and that its metaphorical elements tend to become 'faded' under frequent use.[23] Thus, when Weisgerber, while conceding that it may not be true in every case, claims that the metaphorical element is nevertheless experienced

[18] See esp. pp. 52, 100, above.
[19] See pp. 83-84, above, and Leisi's discussion of the structure of 'word content' in English and German, pp. 89-92, above, which Weisgerber endorses.
[20] See p. 84, above.
[21] See also Roger Brown, *Words and Things* (Glencoe, Ill., 1958), 231.
[22] See esp. pp. 81-82, 98 ff., above.
[23] See Lenneberg (1953), 465-66; Brown, 142, 241-43.

in most of the mountain terms investigated by Zinsli [24] and in words exemplifying the 'concreteness' of German as opposed to the 'abstractness' of French,[25] we must object even under this stipulation. While it is true that the primary etymologies of such words are probably experienced when the latter are first introduced into the language, these experiences gradually disappear as the words are used repeatedly. Metaphors which are of little vitality may appear quite striking to an outside observer, and Greenberg has pointed out the irony in Weisgerber's criticism of Bally for attaching too great an importance to certain expressions,[26] a procedure of which Weisgerber himself is guilty.

The assumption that words represent hypostatized cores of 'meaning' or 'content' is a reflection of the widespread belief in a dualism between mind and body or between a mental realm and a physical realm. But that such a belief is untenable has been shown recently by philosophers and linguists alike.[27] Recognition of the fact that the meaning of a word cannot possibly correspond to a fixed entity but must rather be interpreted as a FUNCTION of its context has given rise to what is variously called the functional, instrumental, or operational theory of linguistic meaning. Wittgenstein, a well-known exponent of this theory, defines meaning in the following way:

For a large class of cases – though not for all – in which we employ the word "meaning" it can be defined thus: the meaning of a word is its use in the language.[28]

In a recent article Haas had restated the instrumentalists' position thus:

[24] See pp. 81-82, above.

[25] See p. 98 ff., above.

[26] Joseph H. Greenberg, "Concerning Inferences from Linguistic to Nonlinguistic Data", in Hoijer (1954), 13. See p. 102, above.

[27] See especially Ludwig Wittgenstein, *Philosophical Investigations,* trans. G. E. M. Anscombe (New York, 1953); Gilbert Ryle, "Ordinary Language", *The Philosophical Review,* LXII (April, 1953), 167-86; Gilbert Ryle, "The Theory of Meaning", in *The Importance of Language* (Englewood Cliffs, N.J., 1962), 147-69; J. R. Firth, *Papers in Linguistics, 1932-1951* (London, 1957), chaps. iii, xiv-xvi.

[28] *Philosophical Investigations,* 20.

The meaning of a word is a collection, an organized recollection, of many individual uses of it, i.e., of various occurrences of it: in verbal and nonverbal contexts, and in positions in which it contrasts with other words. Meaning (like skill) is an "acquired property." Whenever a word is being used significantly, another use is added to remembered uses of it; a present context joins the previous ones.[29]

But, Haas cautions, we should not confuse the 'use of an expression' with denotation, with referring to 'bare' extralingual things, whether in physical or spiritual space.[30] The assumption that a word has a fixed meaning derives from what Haas calls the fiction of isolated reference. But, he writes:

The theory of isolated reference is clearly not meant to be put to the test of observation. It is *in principle* unverifiable. Whatever experience we have of referring to external things, or to ideas, is not an experience of isolated reference. So far from *explaining* the meanings of expressions – even of the referring type – reference *presupposes* a language of significant expressions. Even very young children asking "What is it called?" do not merely refer to, they can tell us a lot about, "it"! For this very reason it interests them. They have already rejected a large number of words as inappropriate to the thing, or they would not ask its name. They have prepared a large number of utterance-frames which the new name will fit into; and where it will join, and contrast with, a large number of other words which already fit those frames. – An "Alsatian"? ... runs, ... barks, ... is big, ... has a thick fur, I don't like ... s, etc. The question "What is it?" or "What is it called?" is *a request to fill in a blank* in an indefinite number of incomplete expressions; it is a request, we might say, for notational help in giving new values to a number of prepared utterance-functions – help in fixing an organization of utterances about a new focal term. Long before it is named, the new thing has already been placed; and it has been contrasted with other things that run or bark, or are big or have a thick fur, are not liked, etc. It has been so placed and contrasted by the help of expressions which were already dealing with it. When I am looking for a word, "have it on the tip of my tongue," this is never a case of some "pure idea" or

---

[29] W. Haas, "The Theory of Translation", *Philosophy*, XXXVII (July, 1962), 213. Cf. also Charles F. Hockett, *A Course in Modern Linguistics* (New York, 1958), 141.

[30] Haas cites "*Geistesraum* [as] being the most serious drawback of some inquiries into 'semantic fields' which are otherwise of considerable interest." He mentions Trier's works specifically. *Ibid.*, 215, n. 1.

"brute fact" begging a name; it is always a case of fragmentary utterances seeking completion. The blank is a variable in a large number of determinate functions; it has a determinate range, and I can already give it many determinate and contrasting values. The variable is the "unknown" in given expressions. But there is no need to interpret it as an imperceptible "soul" searching for its body, or a "thing in itself" wanting a label.[31]

The practice of ascribing to words 'values' that are determined by the 'values' of other words in a given conceptual 'field' and of equating concepts with individual words has often led the Humboldtians to adopt a gratuitous determinism. Thus Weisgerber seems to assume that we can 'recognize' only those objects and events for which we possess individual words.[32] But the fact that a person does not have a word in his vocabulary for some object or event, or for that matter even if his language does not have the word, does not mean that he does not or cannot possess the concept of it. Thus, Black, in criticizing Whorf for the latter's contention that language generates a 'conceptual system', writes:

If we were to accept the view that reference to somebody's-having-a-concept-of-something is a compendious way of talking about certain related capacities to distinguish objects, to respond to them differently, and especially to talk about them [See H. H. Price, *Thinking and Experience* (London, 1953), especially pp. 337-57], we might agree to regard "thinking as the [a?] function which is largely linguistic." But having-a-concept cannot be straightforwardly identified with ability to use the corresponding word.

We must admit that human beings have far more concepts (distinctive cognitive capacities) than words for expressing them – as the example of colors amply shows. Even if symbolization is essential to thought, a place must be left for *ad hoc* symbols, nonverbal tokens, and other ways of thinking without using dictionary words.

Consequently, inferences from vocabulary to cognitive capacities are always precarious. If the presence of a word actively in use suggests the existence of a corresponding concept, absence of a word shows almost nothing.[33]

---

[31]   *Ibid.*, 216-17.
[32]   See p. 54 ff., above.
[33]   Max Black, "Linguistic Relativity: The Views of Benjamin Lee Whorf", *The Philosophical Review*, XLVIII (April, 1959), 231-32. The suggested emendation of Whorf's statement is Black's. Whorf's original quote appears in Whorf (1956), 66.

Even if we were to agree that most of our conceptual thinking consists in 'operating with words',[34] this does not mean that we must have SINGLE words with which to express concepts. We can after all express the latter by means of extended verbal phrases.

In psychological terms, we can describe the process by which a person comes into possession of a given word in his language as one in which, besides learning that it is used in certain specific utterance frames and is excluded from others, he learns to recognize, under the reinforcing influence of his speech community, the criterial attributes of the denotata to which the word applies. We might expect that once a person has learned to recognize these critical attributes, a disposition to attend to them and to ignore other attributes possessed by the denotata would be effected whenever he uses the word. Thus, Henle writes:

It would seem then to be consistent with what we know of mental set on other grounds to assume that the world appears different to a person using one vocabulary than it would to a person using another. The use of language would call attention to different aspects of the environment in the one case than it would in the other. Numerous illustrations of this sort may be given. The Navaho, for example, possess color terms corresponding roughly to our "white," "red," and "yellow" but none which are equivalent to our "black," "gray," "brown," "blue," and "green." They have two terms corresponding to "black," one denoting the black of darkness, the other the black of such objects as coal. Our "gray" and "brown," however, correspond to a single term in their language and likewise our "blue" and "green." As far as vocabulary is concerned, they divide the spectrum into segments different from ours. It would seem probable that on many occasions of casual perception they would not bother to notice whether an object were brown or gray, and that they would merely avoid discussions as to whether a shade of color in a trying light was blue or green, but they would not even make the distinction.[35]

[34]   Ryle (1953), 185.
[35]   Paul Henle, "Language, Thought, and Culture", in *Language, Thought, and Culture*, ed. Paul Henle (Ann Arbor, 1958), 7. On criterial attributes see Jerome S. Bruner, Jacqueline J. Goodnow, and George A. Austin, *A Study of Thinking* (New York, 1956), 30-33 *et passim*. Brown believes that when one comes to understand a linguistic form "his nervous system is partially rewired (in the sense of changes in synaptic resistances or neurone process growth) so that one is disposed to behave appropriately

However, as Henle points out, this does not mean that the Navahos are incapable of making color distinctions which we make, but rather "that their vocabulary tends to let them leave other distinctions unnoticed which we habitually make".[36] Nor does this say anything about the capacity of the Navaho language to express color distinctions which its vocabulary does not habitually make. If he wishes to express such distinctions, the Navaho can probably do so by means of compounds or other extended verbal phrases.

Similarly, Trier's contention that, because thirteenth-century German did not have a word to express pure intelligence divorced from all social connotations, this distinction could not be made [37] must be challenged. The lack of a word expressing this distinction probably merely indicates that the speakers of German at that time did not usually make the distinction.

Brown, in generalizing Zipf's Law, which states that in some languages there is a tendency for the length of a word to be negatively correlated with its frequency of usage, proposes "that the length of a verbal expression (*codability*) provides an index of its frequency in speech, and that this, in turn, is an index of the frequency with which the relevant judgments of difference and equivalence are made". This would mean that speakers of a language which has a single-word expression for a given category would distinguish this category more often than speakers of a language do which must express the category by means of an extended phrase. Brown goes further and proposes "that a perceptual category that is frequently utilized is more available than one less frequently utilized".[38]

---

with regard to that form." Brown, 103. Others who treat meaning as a behavior disposition are Charles L. Stevenson, *Ethics and Language* (New Haven, 1944), and Charles Morris, *Signs, Language and Behavior* (New York, 1946).

[36] *Ibid.*, 8.

[37] See p. 70, above. Raymond Gastil agrees with Trier on this point in his article "Relative Linguistic Determinism", *Anthropological Linguistics*, I (December, 1959), 27-28.

[38] Brown, 235-41; cf. also Brown and Lenneberg, "A Study in Language and Cognition", *Journal of Abnormal and Social Psychology*, XLIX (1954), 454-62. See also Joshua A. Fishman's discussion of the German word

When we come to Weisgerber's discussion of the 'parts of speech' we encounter the same disregard, evinced earlier with regard to individual vocabulary items, of the role played by context. Thus, Weisgerber, though recognizing that many different kinds of 'things', 'activities', and 'qualities' are included within the categories of noun, verb, and adjective, nevertheless believes that there is, however difficult it is to describe, SOME semantic correlate common to each class.[39] However, there is some danger here, as elsewhere, for the student of language to attribute too much to the speaker's consciousness, forgetting that, in ordinary everyday activities, such meanings probably seldom occur to speaker or listener when words are used in typical contexts.[40] As Hockett says: "The impact of inherited linguistic pattern on activities is, in general, least important in the most practical contexts, and most important in such goings-on as story-telling, religion, and philosophizing. . . ."[41]

The distinction Hockett makes here between practical and non-practical contexts is important. The Oxford University professor of philosophy, Gilbert Ryle, makes the same distinction in proclaiming that one of the major functions of philosophy is to clarify the meanings of ordinary language. In his article "Systematically Misleading Expressions" he states that:

Gemütlichkeit in his article "A Systematization of the Whorfian Hypothesis", *Behavioral Science*, V (October, 1960), 327.

[39] See p. 92, above. In another place, p. 98, above, it will be recalled, Weisgerber cites with approval Whorf's claim that, from the supposed fact that "our [that is, the English] normal sentence" contains a subject before the verb, "we therefore read action into every sentence, even into 'I hold it'". To this Max Black answers: "But what is it to 'read' action into a sentence? Can it be anything more than *using* the transitive verb? One formal mark of an 'action' in the narrow sense is the possibility of adding distinctive modifiers: a man may strike (to use Whorf's example) slowly, jerkily, energetically, and so on. Now if somebody were to attach these adverbs to the verb 'to hold' that would be sufficient indication that he was 'reading action' into the verb. I suppose a child might say he was holding his hat slowly, and the poet is allowed a similar license; but otherwise the conceptual confusion is too gross to occur." Black, 234-35.

[40] This applies also to Leisi's concept of hypostatization; see 119ff.

[41] Charles F. Hockett, "Chinese versus English: An Exploration of the Whorfian Thesis", in Hoijer (1954), 123.

There are many expressions which occur in non-philosophical discourse which, though they are perfectly clearly understood by those who use them and those who hear and read them are nevertheless couched in grammatical or syntactial forms which are in a demonstrable way *improper* to the states of affairs which they record. . . . Such expressions can be reformulated and for philosophy but *not* for non-philosophical discourse must be reformulated into expressions of which the syntactical form is proper to the facts recorded. . . . When an expression is of such a syntactical form that it is improper to the fact recorded, it is systematically misleading in that it naturally suggests to some people – though not to "ordinary" people – that the state of affairs recorded is quite a different sort of state of affairs from that which it in fact is.[42]

Ryle distinguishes between three types of statement that are systematically misleading. Of these, the second, quasi-Platonic statements (statements about universals), is especially relevant to the present discussion. Ryle says that when we use expressions like 'Unpunctuality is reprehensible' and 'Virtue is its own reward', it is almost as though we were saying something like 'Jones merits reproof' and 'Smith has given himself the prize'. Thus:

Philosophers, taking it that what is meant by such statements as the former is precisely analogous to what is meant by such statements as the latter, have accepted the consequence that the world contains at least two sorts of objects, namely, particulars like Jones and Smith, and "universals" like Unpunctuality and Virtue.[43]

As Ryle points out, it is absurd to speak of a universal meriting reproof or receiving a reward. What we really mean is 'Whoever is unpunctual deserves that other people should reprove him for being unpunctual' and 'Whoever is good, gains something by being good'. But, Ryle notes, the plain man who uses such quasi-Platonic expression is not making a philosophical mistake:

He is not philosophizing at all. He is not misled by and does not even notice the fraudulent pretense contained in such propositions that

---

[42] *Proceedings of the Aristotelian Society*, XXXII (1931-32), 139-70 (reprinted in *Logic and Language*, First Series, ed. Antony Flew [Oxford, 1952]). Subsequent quotations will be taken from the Flew volume.
[43] Ryle (1952), 20.

they are "about Honesty" or "about Progress." He knows what he means and will, very likely, accept our more formally proper restatement of what he means as a fair paraphrase, but he will not have any motive for desiring the more proper form of expression, nor even any grounds for holding that it is more proper. For he is not attending to the form of the fact in abstraction from the special subject-matter that the fact is about.[44]

Similarly, what we have just said about 'things', 'activities', and 'qualities' being shaped differently according to the context in which they are embedded applies equally well to the differences in the way the various languages classify the same phenomenon as, say, a 'thing' in one language and an 'activity' or 'event' in another. Thus Hartmann's description, approvingly quoted by Weisgerber,[45] of the different cognitive states (because *seeing* is 'verbal' in German and 'nominal' in Japanese) experienced by the mature speaker of Japanese and that experienced by the speaker of German in confronting the same phenomenon must be questioned. Nevertheless, Brown has shown that, however negligible form-class semantic may be in the typical, everyday activities of adult speakers who use words they are familiar with, it is important in the learning of unfamiliar words. He observes that a word is ordinarily introduced in a grammatical context that makes its part-of-speech membership clear: 'Look at the dog' or 'See him running'. From this Brown suggests:

If a part of speech has reliable semantic implications it could call attention to the kind of attribute likely to belong to the meaning of the word. A child who had absorbed the semantics of the noun and verb would know the first time he heard the word *dog* that it was likely to refer to an object having characteristic size and shape whereas running would be likely to name some animal motion.[46]

Brown performed an experiment to see whether preschool children would use the part-of-speech membership of invented words as an aid in discovering the referents of the words. It was found that particular nouns directed attention to objects in a

[44] *Ibid.*, 22.
[45] See p. 93,, above.
[46] Brown, 249.

picture, that mass nouns directed attention to substances, and verbs to actions.[47] Brown reached the following conclusions:

Even though form-class semantic is used in the language learning of both children and adults it probably drops from consciousness as language skills become smooth and rapid. There is no need to think of the moon as feminine when one says "*la lune*," or of charity as a thing, or lightning as an event of brief duration. There is no functional reason to do so, no introspective evidence that one does so, and scarcely enough time in fluent speech for such thought to be possible. However, it does not follow that form-class semantic is inoperative in the accomplished speaker. Like other sorts of meaning it may exist as a disposition. Speakers of Hopi may be prone to think in terms of event-duration when the circumstances are right. They may be more prone to think along these lines than the speaker of English who is placed in like circumstances. Form-class semantic may leave its traces in the nervous system, facilitating thought in some directions, inhibiting thought in other directions. It is not that people are always thinking in terms of gender or substance or round objects, but that they are disposed to think in these terms. The different dispositions should come out in problem solving, poetry writing, painting, and creative thought in general. The effect of form-class semantic cannot be demonstrated with linguistic data alone but requires the study of extra-linguistic behavioral data.[48]

The danger of attaching too great a significance for cognition to individual words and word classes is present also with regard to specific grammatical categories. Thus when Weisgerber declares that the grammatical category of gender in German is "a very important means for the construction of our sentences", "for the continuation of a sequence of thought from one sentence to another", and that "a comparison with the capabilities of languages behaving otherwise is very instructive for realizing the effect of these characteristics",[49] he is implying that the presence of the grammatical category of gender in a language is an advantage measured according to some absolute scale, and that a language not possessing this grammatical feature is lacking in expressive

[47]   See his "Linguistic Determinism and the Part of Speech", *Journal of Abnormal and Social Psychology*, LV (1957), 1-5; see also Brown (1958), 247-53.

[48]   Brown (1958), 253.

[49]   See p. 94, above.

ability. But the assumption of such a scale is completely unwarranted. Every language has its own means of expressing grammatical relationships, and no one has yet been able to demonstrate empirically that the grammatical resources of one language are superior to those of another in the expression of ideas.

Similarly, no valid conclusions concerning cognition can be drawn from inspecting the ORDER in which grammatical elements appear. When Weisgerber asserts that, with the device of incapsulation in German grammar, "the attention cannot wander or roam around at will" and that "the sequence of thoughts cannot be broken off at any place",[50] this reduces to saying that if a speaker or writer of German chooses to express himself by means of the device of incapsulation, he must observe certain rules of grammar. It does NOT prove that the rules of grammar influences his thinking. Moreover, that the speaker's or writer's thinking is not influenced by his language's grammar is implied by Weisgerber himself when he says that, refering to the sentence on p. 95 above, "the thought must be surveyed in its principal features and structured in its full development, before the filling in of the sentence scheme can begin".

The conclusion reached in this study is that the Neo-Humboldtians' position with regard to linguistic relativity cannot withstand serious analysis. This is due ultimately to their almost exclusive reliance on the translation method, that of merely comparing the vocabularies and grammatical structures of different languages. The patent circularity of claiming that thought processes are different among speakers of different languages, and of appealing to linguistic facts alone to demonstrate the truth of this claim has already been discussed in some detail by Lenneberg in connection with Whorf's method.[51]

It is now generally agreed that the following two steps are necessary if we are to make advances in this area. First, the general proposition itself must be stated in explicit, researchable terms and each of the latter carefully defined. Secondly, evidence

[50] See p. 96, above.
[51] Lenneberg (1953).

of an experimental sort must be put forth. That is, to show that the speakers of a given language 'think' differently from the speakers of other languages, it is necessary to appeal ultimately to nonlinguistic facts. Brown, for example, in summarizing the investigations of American ethnolinguists in this area, has suggested that 'language' be defined so as to include semantics, and 'thought' be defined 'in terms of some nonlinguistic behavior'. The thesis here would be "that some nonlinguistic evidence covaries with some linguistic evidence".[52] Without some such approach as this, it is difficult to see how questions of linguistic relativity can be regarded as conclusively settled.[53]

[52]   Brown (1958), 262.
[53]   At least one large-scale research project, the Southwestern Project in Comparative Psycholinguistics, is at present engaged in exploring the Whorfian hypothesis. But so far its findings have been inconclusive. Concerning this and other projects, John Carroll recently writes: "To sum things up, the linguistic-relativity hypothesis has thus far received very little convincing support. Our best guess at present is that the effects of language structure will be found to be limited and localized." *Language and Thought* (Englewood Cliffs, N.J., 1964), 110.

SELECTED BIBLIOGRAPHY [1]

Baldinger, Kurt, *Kollektivsuffixe und Kollektivbegriff* (Berlin, Akademie-verlag, 1950).

Bally, Charles, *Linguistique générale et linguistique française* (Paris, Librairie Ernst Leroux, 1932).

Basilius, Harold, "Neo-Humboldtian Ethnolinguistics", *Word*, VIII (August, 1952), 95-105.

——, "A Structuralist View of German Syntax", *Modern Language Journal*, XXXVII (March, 1953), 130-34.

Bedau, H. A., Review of J. B. Carroll (ed.), *Language, Thought, and Reality* in *Philosophy of Science*, XXIV (1957), 289-93.

Bertalanffy, Ludwig von, "An Essay on the Relativity of Categories", *Philosophy of Science*, XXII (October, 1955), 243-63.

Black, Max, "Linguistic Relativity: The Views of Benjamin Lee Whorf", *The Philosophical Review*, XLVIII (April, 1959), 228-37.

Blanke, Fritz, "Gottessprache und Menschensprache bei J. G. Hamann", *Theologische Blätter*, IX, No. 8 (August, 1930), cols. 201-10.

Brinkmann, Hennig, "Die Wortarten im Deutschen", *Wirkendes Wort*, I (1950), 65-79.

——, "Der deutsche Satz als sprachliche Gestalt", *Wirkendes Wort*, 1. Sonderheft (1952), 12-26.

Brown, Roger, "Linguistic Determinism and the Part of Speech", *Journal of Abnormal and Social Psychology*, LV (1957), 1-5.

——, *Words and Things* (Glencoe, Ill., The Free Press, 1958).

Brown, Roger, and Lenneberg, Eric H., "A Study in Language and Cognition", *Journal of Abnormal and Social Psychology*, XLIX (1954), 454-62.

Bruner, Jerome S., Goodnow, Jacqueline J., and Austin, George A., *A Study of Thinking* (New York, John Wiley and Sons, Inc., 1956).

Carroll, John B., "Linguistic Relativity, Contrastive Linguistics, and Language Learning", *International Review of Applied Linguistics in Language Teaching*, I (1963), 1-20.

——, *Language and Thought* (Englewood Cliffs, N.J., Prentice-Hall, Inc., 1964).

Carroll, John B., and Casagrande, Joseph B., "The Function of Language

[1]   Only those works cited or referred to in text or notes are included.

Classifications in Behavior", in *Readings in Social Psychology*, edited by Eleanor Maccoby, Theodore M. Newcomb, and Eugene L. Hartley (3rd edition, New York, Holt, Rinehart and Winston, Inc., 1958), 18-31.

Casagrande, Joseph B., "The Southwest Project in Comparative Psycholinguistics: A Preliminary Report", in *Men and Cultures*, edited by Anthony F. C. Wallace (Philadelphia, University of Pennsylvania Press, 1960), 777-82.

Cassirer, Ernst, "Die Kantischen Elemente in Wilhelm von Humboldts Sprachphilosophie", *Festschrift für Paul Hensel* (Greiz i.V., Ohag, 1923), 105-27.

——, "Structuralism in Modern Linguistics", *Word*, I (August, 1945), 99-120.

——, *The Philosophy of Symbolic Forms*, translated by Ralph Manheim, Vol. I (New Haven, Yale University Press, 1953).

Drach, Erich, *Grundgedanken der deutschen Satzlehre* (Frankfurt am Main, Moritz Diesterweg, 1937).

Ducháček, O., "Les champs linguistiques", *Philologica Pragensia*, III (1960), 22-35.

Feuer, Lewis S., "Sociological Aspects of the Relation between Language and Philosophy", *Philosophy of Science*, XX (April, 1953), 85-100.

Finck, Franz Nikolaus, *Der deutsche Sprachbau als Ausdruck deutscher Weltanschauung* (Marburg, N. G. Elwert'sche Verlagsbuchhandlung, 1899).

Firth, J. R., Preliminary Report in *Proceedings of the Seventh International Congress of Linguists* (London, The Seventh International Congress of Linguists, 1956), 5-9.

——, *Papers in Linguistics, 1932-1951* (London, Oxford University Press, 1957).

Fishman, Joshua A., "A Systematization of the Whorfian Hypothesis", *Behavioral Science*, V (October, 1960), 323-39.

Flavell, J. H., "A Test of the Whorfian Hypothesis", *Psychological Reports*, IV (1958), 455-62.

Gastil, Raymond D., "Relative Linguistic Determinism", *Anthropological Linguistics*, I (December, 1959), 24-38.

Gelb, A., and Goldstein, K., "Über Farbennamenamnesie", *Psychologische Forschung*, VI (1925), 127-86.

Glinz, Hans, *Die innere Form des Deutschen* (2d ed. revised, Bern, Francke Verlag, 1961).

Goldstein, Kurt, "On Naming and Pseudonaming, from Experiences in Psychopathology", *Word*, II (April, 1946), 1-7.

——, *Language and Language Disturbances* (New York, Grune and Stratton, 1948).

Greenberg, Joseph H., "Concerning Inferences from Linguistic to Nonlinguistic Data", in *Language in Culture*, edited by H. Hoijer (Chicago, University of Chicago Press, 1954), 3-19.

Gründer, Karlfried, *Figur und Geschichte: Johann Georg Hamanns*

"Biblische Betrachtungen" als Ansatz einer Geschichtsphilosophie (Freiburg, Verlag Karl Alber, 1958).

Haas, W., "The Theory of Translation", *Philosophy*, XXXVII (July, 1962), 208-28.

Hamann, Johann Georg, *Schriften*, edited by Friedrich Roth and G. A. Wiener, 8 vols (Berlin, G. Reimer, 1821-43).

——, *Briefwechsel mit Friedrich Heinrich Jacobi*, edited by C. H. Gildemeister, Vol. V (Gotha, Friedrich Andreas Perthes, 1868).

——, *Sämtliche Werke*, edited by Josef Nadler, 6 vols. (Vienna, Verlag Herder, 1949-57).

Hartmann, Peter, *Einige Grundzüge des japanischen Sprachbaues* (Heidelberg, C. Winter Universitätsverlag, 1952).

——, *Wesen und Wirkung der Sprache im Spiegel der Theorie Leo Weisgerbers* (Heidelberg, C. Winter Universitätsverlag, 1958).

Haym, Rudolf, *Wilhelm von Humboldt: Lebensbild und Charakteristik* (Berlin, Verlag von Rudolph Gaertner, 1856).

——, *Herder nach seinem Leben und seinen Werken*, Vol. I (Berlin, Verlag von Rudolph Gaertner, 1877).

Heinemann, Fritz, *Wilhelm v. Humboldts Philosophische Anthropologie und Theorie der Menschenkenntnis* (Halle/Salle, Max Niemeyer Verlag, 1929).

Henle, Paul, "Language, Thought, and Culture", in *Language, Thought, and Culture*, edited by Paul Henle (Ann Arbor, The University of Michigan Press, 1958), 1-24.

Herder, Johann Gottfried, *Sämtliche Werke*, edited by Bernhard Suphan, 33 vols. (Berlin, Weidmannsche Buchhandlung, 1877-1913).

Hockett, Charles F., "Chinese versus English: An Exploration of the Whorfian Thesis", in *Language in Culture*, edited by H. Hoijer (Chicago, University of Chicago Press, 1954), 106-23.

——, *A Course in Modern Linguistics* (New York, Macmillan Co., 1958).

Hoijer, Harry (ed.), *Language in Culture: Proceedings of a Conference on the Interrelations of Language and Other Aspects of Culture* (Chicago, University of Chicago Press, 1954).

Humboldt, Wilhelm von, *Gesammelte Schriften*, edited by Albert Leitzmann, 7 vols. (Berlin, B. Behrs Verlag, 1903-1918).

Humphrey, George, *Thinking: An Introduction to Its Experimental Psychology* (New York, John Wiley and Sons, 1951).

Husserl, Edmund, *Logische Untersuchungen*, Vol. II (2d ed. revised, Halle, Max Niemeyer Verlag, 1921).

Ipsen, Gunter, "Der alte Orient und die Indogermanen", in *Stand und Aufgaben der Sprachwissenschaft: Festschrift für W. Streitberg* (Heidelberg, C. Winters Universitätsbuchhandlung, 1924), 200-37.

——, "Der neue Sprachbegriff", *Zeitschrift für Deutschkunde*, XLVI, No. 1 (1932), 1-18.

——, *Sprachphilosophie der Gegenwart* (Berlin, Junker und Dünnhaupt Verlag, 1930).

Jespersen, Otto, *The Philosophy of Grammar* (New York, Henry Holt and Co., 1924).

Jolles, A., "Antike Bedeutungsfelder", *Beiträge zur Geschichte der deutschen Sprache und Literatur*, LVIII (1934), 97-109.

Jost, Leonhard, *Sprache als Werk und wirkende Kraft: Ein Beitrag zur Geschichte und Kritik der energetischen Sprachauffassung seit Wilhelm von Humboldt* (*Sprache und Dichtung*, 6) (Bern, Haupt, 1960).

Kronasser, Heinz, *Handbuch der Semasiologie: Kurze Einführung in die Geschichte, Problematik und Terminologie der Bedeutungslehre* (Heidelberg, C. Winter Universitätsverlag, 1952).

Langen, August, "Deutsche Sprachgeschichte vom Barock bis zur Gegenwart", in *Deutsche Philologie im Aufriss*, edited by Wolfgang Stammler, Vol. I (Berlin, Erich Schmidt Verlag, 1952), cols. 931-1396.

Lees, Robert B., Review of Noam Chomsky's *Syntactic Structures*, in *Language*, XXXIII (July-September, 1957), 375-408.

Leibnitz, Gottfried Wilhelm, *The Monadology*, translated by R. Latta and G. M. Duncan (London, Favil Press, 1930).

Leisi, Ernst, *Der Wortinhalt: Seine Struktur im Deutschen und Englischen* (2d ed. revised, Heidelberg, Quelle & Meyer, 1961).

Lenneberg, Eric H., "Cognition in Ethnolinguistics", *Language*, XXIX (July-September, 1953), 463-71.

——, "A Note on Cassirer's Philosophy of Language", *Philosophy and Phenomenological Research*, XV (June, 1955), 512-22.

Lenneberg, Eric H., and Roberts, J. M., *The Language of Experience* (*Indiana University Publications in Anthropology and Linguistics, Memoir* 13) (Baltimore, Waverly Press, 1956).

Lévi-Strauss, Claude, Jakobson, Roman, Voegelin, C. F., and Sebeok, Thomas, *Results of the Conference of Anthropologists and Linguists* (*Indiana University Publications in Anthropology and Linguistics, Memoir* 8) (Baltimore, Waverly Press, 1953).

Longacre, Robert E., Review of Wilbur M. Urban's *Language and Reality* and Benjamin Lee Whorf's *Four Articles on Metalinguistics*, in *Language*, XXXII (April-June, 1956), 298-308.

Lovejoy, Arthur O., *The Great Chain of Being: A Study of the History of an Idea* (Cambridge, Mass., Harvard University Press, 1936).

——, "The Meaning of Romanticism for the Historian of Ideas", *Journal of the History of Ideas*, II (June, 1941), 272-78.

Metzke, Erwin, *J. G. Hamanns Stellung in der Philosophie des 18. Jahrhunderts* (Halle/Salle, Max Niemeyer Verlag, 1934).

Meyer, Richard M., "Die militärischen Titel", *Zeitschrift für Deutsche Wortforschung*, XII (1910), 145-56.

Miller, George A., *Language and Communication* (New York, McGraw-Hill Book Co., Inc., 1951).

Morris, Charles, *Signs, Language and Behavior* (New York, Prentice-Hall, 1946).

Moulton, William G., Review of Hans Glinz's *Die innere Form des Deutschen*, in *Language*, XXIX (April-June, 1953), 175-80.

O'Flaherty, James C., *Unity and Language: A Study in the Philosophy of Johann Georg Hamann* (*University of North Carolina Studies in the Germanic Languages and Literatures*, No. 6) (Chapel Hill, University of North Carolina, 1952).

Öhman, Suzanne, *Wortinhalt und Weltbild: Vergleichende und methodologische Studien zu Bedeutungslehre und Wortfeldtheorie* (Stockholm, Kungl. Boktryckeriet P. A. Norstedt & Söner, 1951).

——, "Theories of the 'Linguistic Field' ", *Word*, IX (August, 1953), 123-34.

Osthoff, Hermann, *Vom Suppletivwesen der indogermanischen Sprachen* (Heidelberg, Universitätsbuchdruckerei von J. Hörning, 1899).

Porzig, Walter, "Der Begriff der inneren Sprachform", *Indogermanische Forschungen*, XLI, No. 2 (1923), 150-69.

——, "Aufgaben der indogermanischen Syntax", in *Stand und Aufgaben der Sprachwissenschaft: Festschrift für W. Streitberg* (Heidelberg. C. Winters Universitätsbuchhandlung, 1924), 126-51.

——, "Wesenhafte Bedeutungsbeziehungen", *Beiträge zur Geschichte der deutschen Sprache und Literatur*, LVIII (1934), 70-97.

——, *Das Wunder der Sprache* (2d ed. revised, Bern, Francke Verlag, 1957).

Price, H. H., *Thinking and Experience* (London, Hutchinson's University Library, 1953).

Radnitzky, G. A., "Some Remarks on the Whorfian Hypothesis", *Behavioral Science*, VI (1961), 153-57.

Ryle, Gilbert, "Systematically Misleading Expressions", in *Logic and Language*, edited by A. Flew, First Series (Oxford, B. Blackwell, 1952).

——, "Ordinary Language", *The Philosophical Review*, LXII (April, 1953), 167-86.

——, "The Theory of Meaning", in *The Importance of Language*, edited by M. Black (Englewood Cliffs, N.J., Prentice-Hall, Inc., 1962), 147-69.

Saussure, Ferdinand de, *Course in General Linguistics*, translated by Wade Baskin (New York, Philosophical Library, 1959).

Scheidweiler, F., "Die Wortfeldtheorie", *Zeitschrift für deutsches Altertum*, LXXIX (1942), 249-72.

Scherer, Wilhelm, *Zur Geschichte der deutschen Sprache* (Berlin, Weidmannsche Buchhandlung, 1868).

Schneider, Theophora, "Der intellektuelle Wortschatz Meister Eckeharts: Ein Beitrag zur Geschichte des deutschen Sprachinhalts." Unpublished Ph.D. dissertation, University of Münster, 1934.

Schwarz, Hans, "Leitmerkmale sprachlicher Felder", in *Sprache – Schlüssel zur Welt: Festschrift für Leo Weisgerber* (Düsseldorf: Pädagogischer Verlag Schwann, 1959), 245-55.

Spence, N. C. W., "Linguistic Fields, Conceptual Systems and the *Weltbild*", *Transactions of the Philological Society* (1961), 87-106.

Stevenson, Charles L., *Ethics and Language* (New Haven, Yale University Press, 1944).

Stöhr, A., *Lehrbuch der Logik in psychologischer Darstellung* (Leipzig, F. Deuticke, 1910).

Stoltenberg, Hans L., *Neue Sprachgestaltung* (Lahr, M. Schauenburg, 1930).

Stroh, Fritz, *Der volkhafte Sprachbegriff* (Halle, Max Niemeyer Verlag, 1933).

——, "Allgemeine Sprachwissenschaft und Sprachphilosophie", *Germanische Philologie: Ergebnisse und Aufgaben: Festschrift für O. Behaghel* (Heidelberg, C. Winters Universitätsbuchhandlung, 1934), 229-42.

Trier, Jost, *Der deutsche Wortschatz im Sinnbezirk des Verstandes: Die Geschichte eines sprachlichen Feldes, I: Von den Anfängen bis zum Beginn des 13. Jahrhunderts* (Heidelberg, C. Winters Universitätsbuchhandlung, 1931).

——, "Sprachliche Felder", *Zeitschrift für deutsche Bildung*, VIII (1932), 417-27.

——, "Das sprachliche Feld", *Neue Jahrbücher für Wissenschaft und Jugendbildung*, X (1934), 428-49.

——, "Deutsche Bedeutungsforschung", in *Germanische Philologie: Ergebnisse und Aufgaben: Festschrift für O. Behaghel* (Heidelberg, C. Winters Universitätsbuchhandlung, 1934), 173-200.

——, "Über die Erforschung des menschenkundlichen Wortschatzes", in *Actes du Quatrième Congrès International des Linguistes* (Copenhagen, E. Munksgaard, 1938), 92-98.

Ullmann, Stephen, *The Principles of Semantics* (2d ed. revised, Oxford, B. Blackwell, 1957).

——, *Semantics: An Introduction to the Science of Meaning* (Oxford, B. Blackwell, 1962).

Unger, Rudolf, *Hamanns Sprachtheorie im Zusammenhange seines Denkens* (Munich, C. H. Beck'sche Verlagsbuchhandlung, 1905).

Urban, Wilbur M., *Language and Reality* (New York, Macmillan Co., 1939).

——, "Cassirer's Philosophy of Language", in *The Philosophy of Ernst Cassirer*, edited by Paul Schilpp (New York, Tudor Publishing Co., 1949), 401-41.

Vossler, Karl, "Volksprachen und Weltsprachen", *Welt und Wort*, I (September, 1946), 97-101.

Wallace, Anthony F. C., and Atkins, John, "The Meaning of Kinship Terms", *American Anthropologist*, LXII (February, 1960), 58-80.

Waterman, John T., "Benjamin Lee Whorf and Linguistic Field-Theory", *Southwestern Journal of Anthropology*, XIII (Autumn, 1957), 201-11.

Weisgerber, Leo, "Das Problem der inneren Sprachform", *Germanisch-Romanische Monatsschrift*, XIV (1926), 241-56.

——, "Die Bedeutungslehre – ein Irrweg der Sprachwissenschaft?", *Germanisch-Romanische Monatsschrift*, XV (1927), 161-83.

——, "Vorschläge zur Methode und Terminologie der Wortforschung", *Indogermanische Forschungen*, XLVI (1928), 305-25.

——, "Adjektivische und verbale Auffassung der Gesichtsempfindungen", *Wörter und Sachen*, XII (1929), 197-226.

——, *Muttersprache und Geistesbildung* (Göttingen, Vandenhoeck & Ruprecht, 1929).

——, "Sprachwissenschaft und Philosophie zum Bedeutungsproblem", *Blätter für deutsche Philosophie*, IV (1930), 17-46.

——, *Von den Kräften der deutschen Sprache* (Düsseldorf, Pädagogischer Verlag Schwann), Vol. I: *Die Sprache unter den Kräften des menschlichen Daseins* (2d ed., 1954); Vol. II: *Vom Weltbild der deutschen Sprache* (1950); 2d ed. revised: 1. Halbband, *Die inhaltbezogene Grammatik* (1953); 2. Halbband, *Die sprachliche Erschliessung der Welt* (1954); Vol. III: *Die Muttersprache im Aufbau unserer Kultur* (2d ed. revised, 1957); Vol. IV: *Die geschichtliche Kraft der deutschen Sprache* (2d ed. revised, 1959).

——, "Relativismus in Humboldts Sprachbetrachtung?", *Das Gespräch: Blätter der Freunde des Pädagogischen Verlags Schwann Düsseldorf*, Ausgabe A, Folge 2 (Frühjahr, 1953), 3-4.

Werner, Heinz, *Die Ursprünge der Metapher* (Leipzig, W. Englemann, 1919).

Whitney, William D., *The Life and Growth of Language* (New York, D. Appleton and Co., 1880).

Whorf, Benjamin Lee, *Language, Thought, and Reality: Selected Writings of Benjamin Lee Whorf*, edited by John B. Carroll (Cambridge, Mass., Mass. Institute of Technology, 1956).

Wittgenstein, Ludwig, *Philosophical Investigations*, translated by G. E. M. Anscombe (New York, Macmillan Co., 1953).

Zinsli, Paul, *Grund und Grad: Die Bergwelt im Spiegel der schweizerdeutschen Alpenmundarten* (Bern, Verlag A. Francke [1946]).

DATE DUE

GAYLORD   PRINTED IN U.S A.